the new
OUTDOOR KITCHEN

the new
OUTDOOR KITCHEN

*Cooking Up a Kitchen for the Way
You Live and Play*

Deborah Krasner with Michael Krasner

Photography by Eric Roth

The Taunton Press

The New Outdoor Kitchen was originally published in hardcover by The Taunton Press, Inc.

The Taunton Press

The Taunton Press, Inc., 63 South Main Street, PO Box 5506, Newtown, CT 06470-5506
e-mail: tp@taunton.com

Editor: Pam Hoenig
Jacket/Cover design: Renato Stanisic, adapted for paperback by Amy Russo
Interior design and layout: Renato Stanisic
Illustrator: Martha Garstang Hill
Photographer: Eric Roth

Library of Congress Cataloging-in-Publication Data

Krasner, Deborah.
  The new outdoor kitchen : cooking up a kitchen for the way you live and play / Deborah Krasner with Michael Krasner ; photographs by Eric Roth.
      p. cm.
  Includes bibliographical references and index.
  ISBN-13: 978-1-56158-804-6 (alk. paper)
  ISBN-13: 978-1-60085-009-7 paperback (alk. paper)
  ISBN-10: 1-56158-804-0 (alk. paper)
  1. Garden structures--Design and construction--Amateurs' manuals. 2. Garden ornaments and furniture--Design and construction--Amateurs' manuals. 3. Outdoor kitchens--Design and construction--Amateurs' manuals. 4. Barbecues (Fireplaces)--Design and construction--Amateurs' manuals. I. Krasner, Michael. II. Title.
  TH4961.K73 2007
  643'.3--dc22
                    2006018103
Printed in Singapore
10 9 8 7 6 5 4 3 2 1

Acknowledgments

A big thank you to editor Pam Hoenig for realizing this was a book that needed to be written, and for inviting me to be its author. Also at The Taunton Press, I thank Katie Benoit for all her hard work. I am grateful for this support, as I am to so many others:

To the Hearth, Patio & Barbecue Association, whose invitation to their annual convention allowed me to learn about so many of the products I write about in this book. Thank you to the Casual Furniture Association, for permission to reprint their guidelines on casual furniture. Many thanks to Donna Myers, who spent weeks fact-checking the chapter on grills and smokers to make sure I didn't say anything inaccurate. Her efforts went beyond anything I could have asked, and I am grateful. Justin Costamagna and the team at Niles Audio took time out to read the sound chapter and offer helpful corrections and warnings. Jack Miller, general manager of landscape lighting for Kichler, made useful comments on the lighting section. Also at Kichler, I want to thank Sid Fleichman for his help in providing the two outdoor wall sconces

on the deck. Cruz Perez of Vista Professional Outdoor Lighting enthusiastically supported the project; Vista actually created a special light to illuminate the interior of the pizza oven, and sent Thomas Petrush to give me hands-on training in designing and installing outdoor lighting. I am immensely grateful. I'm grateful too to Velux's Keith Hobbs, who sent Shawn Oxford to clarify installation requirements for locating skylights in the path of snow. Glenn Bowman generously sent Matt and John from Vermont Soapstone, who went well out of their way to do an incredible installation of the soapstone counters and backsplash. Victor Jillson, from Merrill Gas, made time in the midst of a great press of work to connect the gas in time for photography.

So many people and manufacturers helped create the demonstration outdoor kitchen and outdoor living spaces that comprise the last section of this book. I am deeply grateful to each of them:

Thank you to Lou West for giving me the chance to cook on a Big Green Egg, big cheers to Justin Newby, Kim Roman, and KitchenAid for your extraordinary generosity and ongoing support for my design work. Thank you to Carter Grandle for your beautiful casual furniture that makes it clear that you can be as stylish and comfortable outdoors as in. Thanks to Glenn Bowman and Vermont Soapstone, for always reminding me that local is better and that soapstone is the best. Thanks also to Chicago Faucet for making a flexible and well-designed wall-mounted articulating faucet that's perfect for any outdoor kitchen; to CookShack, for teaching me about the thrills of electric smoke; and to Fogazzo Ovens, whose enthusiasm and generosity make the outdoor kitchen sing in Italian. TealCedar make the beautiful cedar shakes that add such great charm to the kitchen pavilion roof. I am enormously grateful to Huck DeVenzio of Wolmanized Lumber, who made it possible to showcase lots of special woodcraft on the entire underdeck and to build the post-and-beam outdoor kitchen pavilion using treated wood. Trex decking and railings enabled us to build a big two-level deck with the confidence that it will last and look good for a very long time. Our local ScreenMobile dealer, Ken Robinson, thoughtfully created a screen porch that can withstand Vermont summers, and did the installation with extraordinary generosity and care. Danver's stainless steel outdoor kitchen cabinets are not only beautiful, they are really made to withstand weather. I am grateful to Mitch Slater for making it possible to put them in the pavilion, and to Deborah Jones and Mike Wallace at Danvers for all their help. Tom Nicolai, one of Chicago's outdoor-kitchen specialists, gave me lots of advice and the chance to try out a Pappa'z Pizza Oven firsthand. Thanks to Campagnia International for those wonderful fiberglass planters that perfectly illustrate how large-scale planters work on a deck; to Krupps (www.krupps.com/wall-fountains) for the fountain that enlivens the wall near the outdoor kitchen; and to Linda at www. weathervanes.com, who made the beautiful cupola with a copper roof that adds such charm and function to the kitchen pavilion. Thanks too to Niles Audio for their great outdoor speakers, and to Velux for flooding the screen porch with light and air with their venting skylight. To the Modern Fan Company, who make beautiful indoor and outdoor fans that are unequaled in their functionality and visual appeal. To Blue Rhino, SkeeterVac, and Endless Summer for the bug killer and tall patio heater. To Connie Bryant at Home Depot, and Paul at our local WW Building Supply in Newfane, Vt., for their support of this project. I'm grateful too for the Ardennes Gray concrete Bergerac pavers on the outdoor kitchen patio —a local product available nationally, they're distributed by Belgard. The folks at Arthur Whitcomb, in Brattleboro, Vt. were our source.

So many friends in the food community offered leads and help in finding locations. I am particularly grateful to Lisa Weiss, Diane Philips, Nick Malgieri, Kathy Gunst, and Amelia Saltzman for their good suggestions, along with all the other foodies who responded to Pam and to my calls for locations and aid. So many people at IACP/ Dallas gave us suggestions that they are too numerous to name, but know that I am so grateful. Thank you too to garden writer Gordon Hayward for his help in pointing the way to the Maryland outdoor kitchen. For making wonderful outdoor kitchens good enough to include in this book I am so appreciative of all the homeowners who presented and styled their outdoor spaces, and then let us photograph them—deep thanks indeed to Peter Bergh, Rick Bayless, Carol Obrecht, Bill and Cheryl Jamison,

Nancy Schwan, Robyn Lee, Gary Peese, Jim and Cindy Schoeneck, Michael McCarty, Lisa Weiss, Emily Luchetti, and Jim Stott and Jonathan King (and to Cynthia Maranhas for all of her help and hard work). Finally, for custom shooting the portfolios that illustrate ten kitchens in depth for this book, I am especially grateful to Eric Roth for his beautiful and deeply informative photographs, and to Sabrina Velandry, Eric's assistant, who worked so hard to make the schedule possible. Rick Bayless's portfolio was shot by Linda Oyama Bryan. I am most grateful to her for such beautiful work.

Many people worked to make the demonstration outdoor rooms of this book come together in actuality and for photography. I am deeply grateful to architect Andy Armstrong for doing such an incredible job in designing the deck, porch, and pavilion, including all of the decorative details that make the finished project so alluring. Jim Spencer of TrueCraft Construction and his crew built the outdoor rooms, anticipating things like the need for screening under the floor of a screen porch. We feel extremely fortunate to have had the help of landscape designer Edwin de Bruijn of Hollands Bloom, who did such a perfect job of creating and integrating the pavilion landscape between the deck and meadow. Peter Welch did the masonry work for the pizza oven with panache and creativity, for which I am most grateful. Hilary Duggan worked on making all the gardens look their best and designed the plantings near the terraces and deck base. Steve Grover made sure that the fields were mowed in time for photography, even as he was about to leave for vacation. In addition, I'm grateful to garden designer Kris Fenderson for his consultation early on in the process, which yielded a big view vision and wonderful planting suggestions.

Friends and fellow authors Michael Daley and Jessie Haas came over to help get the project ready for photography, and lent their considerable skills to putting things together under pressure. Jill Hulme's plants and planters made even an autumn garden look splendid and Hilary Duggan styled those plants for photography, making them fit lushly into the landscape.

During the process of writing each of my previous books, my nearest and dearest have always been supportive. On this project, however, two of them went well beyond support. My husband, Michael Krasner, did much of the research for the grill section, becoming in the process an expert on equipment and outdoor cooking. He also functioned yet again as my in-house editor, bringing his clear vision and uncommon good sense to issues of writing and editing. Garden writer Cecile Shapiro, who I am happy to reveal is also my mother, wrote some of the sidebars in the Planting section, adding her many years of garden-writing experience and deep understanding of plant materials to enrich the book.

Contents

Welcome to the Pleasures of the Outdoor Kitchen 2

Welcome to the Pleasures
of the Outdoor Kitchen

Whether you live in a climate where outdoor living is possible for most of the year, or, as I do, in a place where spring and summer merge into a bare three-month-long window, cooking and dining outside has enormous appeal. Although lean-to "summer kitchens" used to be built outdoors to keep the house cool, these days we all want to cook and live outside for the sheer pleasure of it.

Living outside—and living well—is the reason for this book. The great suburban migration of the mid-20th century produced outdoor kitchens furnished with modest barbecues and wooden picnic tables, but our standards and aspirations have grown into a desire for outdoor kitchens and dining areas that match our homes in quality, style, performance, and attractiveness.

Manufacturers have taken note. These days, the equipment available for outdoor living includes restaurant-level high-BTU gas grills; outdoor refrigerators; sinks of all styles and sizes; task and ambient lighting; stone, tile, and cast-cement counters the equal of their interior kitchen cousins; and

ovens up to the job of cooking everything from bread and pizza to a whole pig. Amenities for outdoor social spaces include portable fireplaces and heaters, outdoor furniture that rivals interior models for comfort and visual appeal, garden structures from gazebos to antique barns, and even carpets and sound systems designed for backyard use.

Confronted by all these possibilities, what is a homeowner to do? Where should you begin? How can you start planning, or researching, or even considering a budget? This book will answer all of your questions. We'll show you lots of great dream material and specific details, but we'll also tell you how to get from dream to reality.

We'll also show you lots of equipment choices, as well as offering information on materials and styles for everything from patio and deck flooring to counters and trellises. We'll give you sources for everything in the book, and websites for designers and manufacturers. But most of all, especially in Chapter 1, we'll give you a map for the design process, showing you how to think through a complete plan.

Your Outdoor Kitchen:
From Dream to Reality

An outdoor kitchen invites you to revel in the pleasures of the natural world. With the incomparable flavor of outdoor cooking, the relaxed comfort of an al fresco setting, the air scented with sweet smoke and illuminated by candlelight, your outdoor kitchen will provide many hours of pleasure to you, your family, and friends.

At its most basic, an outdoor kitchen is a place to cook and eat out of doors. It can be located on a screened-in porch or on a patio; it can be set in a courtyard or out in the garden; it can be in a meadow, on a beach, or in any spot beyond your back door. An outdoor kitchen can be temporary and lit by torches, with food cooked on a portable grill and served on a wooden table you've brought from indoors, or it can be a permanent

FACING PAGE: Tiki torches define the corners of this temporary outdoor dining room. Indoor furniture, an attractive tablecloth, fine glasses, and china set an elegant tone. Glass hurricane shades shelter candles from breezes.

installation, equipped with a built-in grill, a wood-fired oven, major appliances, and electric and gas hookups. Between those two extremes exists a world of possibilities.

Getting Your Dream Kitchen: Beginning the Process

The first step is to develop a clear picture of what you want. You can begin with something quite modest, like a patio with a store-bought grill, while planning for growth over time into something quite wonderful. You can also start modest and stay there, creating an intimate outdoor kitchen that suits your particular needs beautifully.

When thinking about what you want, it helps to ask the following two questions:

How do you intend to use your outdoor kitchen?

Are you going to use your outdoor kitchen throughout the year, during the week as well as on the weekend? The more ambitious

This outdoor kitchen features lots of counter space and a shaded area for dining. Even though it's located close to the indoor kitchen, it still has its own sink and storage for pots and pans and foodstuffs.

A Catered Affair from Your Outdoor Kitchen

If you think there might be an outdoor catered event in your future, consider building some caterer-friendly features into your outdoor kitchen if at all possible. Sharon Myers, of Sharon Myers Fine Catering in southern Vermont, suggests the following:

Make sure the outdoor kitchen has lots of electrical outlets, good lighting, as much counter space as possible, running water (even if only cold), and a nearby place to hide both catering equipment and another portable cooking spot, if necessary. Caterers arrive with large numbers of heavy coolers filled with food and need a place to store them and keep them cool. You might even want to create a half-hidden alcove (using screens or plantings) outside of any traffic pattern and near the cooking area that can hold excess equipment and/or function as an auxiliary kitchen or staging area.

your cooking is, the more space you'll need for equipment, preparation, and that critical comfort component, a place to hang out while you wait for the food to cook.

Do you plan to do most of your food preparation work indoors or out in the yard? If you are prepping food outside, you'll want counter space and refrigeration. Will the whole family be cooking, or is just one of you the outdoor cook? You may want to build in seating if you often have lots of company as you cook, and consider making separate work stations if you have help in the kitchen. Is this going to be an occasional party space or an every night family dinner spot? If it's made for parties, you'll need to plan lots of counter space and many electrical outlets; for family dinners, you'll want a close-by eating area. Do you think you might be using this space

Though large in scale, this ell-shaped permanent outdoor kitchen fits seamlessly into its surroundings. The built-in grill is set away from the dining area and house to minimize smoke, and the massive raised brick fireplace provides heat and a focal point. A matching brick floor helps to define and unify the whole area.

for catered events? See "A Catered Affair from Your Outdoor Kitchen" for possible features you might want to consider in the planning stages to make your kitchen caterer-friendly.

If your patio parties aren't complete without the whir of the blender whipping up frozen drinks, then maybe you'll want a separate bar area, complete with a refrigerator and icemaker. If you want to be able to use this space year-round, you'll most likely need a heater. Your refrigerator and icemaker will need electrical power outlets; a heater can be electric or gas powered.

How big and permanent a setup do you want?

You also need to consider scale: Perhaps you want a large built-in cooking area with seating and/or cooking stations for guests and an even larger dining area. Or it could be that your available space dictates a freestanding grill station and a cozy dining area. Or maybe you're somewhere in the middle,

with hopes of a built-in grill, a sink connected to a hose, and a basic electrical setup.

Each of these alternatives comes with a very different price tag. For example, a permanent outdoor kitchen equipped with an outdoor fireplace, wood-burning oven, built-in gas grill with side burners, refrigerator, sink with hot and cold water, natural-gas lines for the grill and for gas-fueled tiki torches, electric lighting systems, finished weatherproof cabinetry, stone counters, and professional landscaping can easily run into six figures.

In contrast, a kitchen with freestanding equipment (a store-bought grill, prefab wood-fired oven, small outdoor under-counter refrigerator, and freestanding sink) can be located on a deck, concrete slab, or sand-supported pavers, with a garden hose sink connected to a French drain (gravel under grass) and a pedestal electric outlet for the utilities. Such an outdoor kitchen can work nearly as well as the first example, at a fraction of the cost.

Your Outdoor Kitchen File

Get a big accordion file, because you're going to be amassing lots of information. Your goal is twofold: to determine what you most like in terms of equipment and style, and to eventually create an overall budget, broken down into equipment costs, material costs, labor costs, and landscaping costs. Start collecting the following:

- Magazine photos of outdoor kitchen setups you like.
- Magazine and catalog photos of cooking equipment, oudoor furniture, and lighting you like.
- Manufacturer brochures of equipment you're considering, plus price lists.
- Names of landscape designers and contractors who do this kind of work, either who come recommended or whose advertisements you've seen.

When making these decisions, it's helpful to consider how long you plan to live at your current address. If you think a move is in your future, construct an outdoor kitchen that can move with you—for a casual cook, a grill on wheels and a portable island for serving, for a more ambitious outdoor chef, a portable wood-fired oven as well as a portable gas grill and smoker. A great entertainer may need the biggest portable grill cart available, fitted with a refrigerator and warming drawer, with a portable icemaker on a big-wheeled restaurant table that offers generous counter space for plating and serving.

Planning for now, planning for later

Everything doesn't have to be done all at once. Be honest with yourself about what your priorities are. If your budget doesn't allow for both, consider which is more important to you, a wood-fired oven or an outdoor fireplace. Will a freestanding fire pit do instead of a fireplace? If a flagstone terrace with surrounding retaining walls is your heart's desire, then perhaps you can

Protected by the walls of the house and garage, this outdoor kitchen is buffered from harsh weather. The vine-covered pergola adds further shelter.

make concessions on equipment, knowing you can upgrade later.

In addition to prioritizing, you also need to plan for the future. If you've planned ahead, you'll be able to step up to an outdoor sink, a built-in gas grill, and an outdoor refrigerator several years later without having to, for example, rip out that flagstone patio because you neglected to lay necessary electric, natural-gas, and water lines under it while it was being built. At the same time, plan for lighting, sound systems, electric heaters, water features (they often require a recirculating pump), and gas-fueled fireplaces or fire pits. Now is the time to dream fully and plan efficiently.

Location, Location, Location

If your yard is tiny and abuts neighbors on both sides, plan your kitchen to minimize the degree to which your noise, smoke, and light will impinge on your neighbors. You also

need to consider your own desire for privacy.

With more land, your choices of possible sites multiply. In this case, issues of transport or preserving or creating views enter the equation. Here too, it's important to keep scale in mind to avoid creating an outdoor space that is either too large or too small for the house it serves.

Think about how a cooking area will impact the look of your yard or garden, both from inside the house and from the street. Also, decide how far or near you want this space to be to your home and its indoor kitchen. There are advantages and disadvantages to both.

Building onto or next to the house
Convenience is the biggest advantage of this scenario, because it will be much simpler (and less expensive) to run water, electricity, and natural gas out to the outdoor kitchen. Transporting food outside will also be easier. When the outdoor kitchen is attached to the house, you can make a pass-through, or use a window as a pass-through, adding even more convenience. In one kitchen I designed, we built a window pass-through as well as an interior underwindow bookcase with a wide ledge at the top covered with zinc sheeting so that it functions as a serving place in the indoor kitchen and a landing place when things are going out to and coming in from the outdoor kitchen.

Another great advantage of an attached outdoor kitchen is that the outdoor space is buffered from weather by the walls of the building. An outdoor kitchen in an ell formed by two wings of a building or in a courtyard protected on three sides by the house, or even an outdoor kitchen that only touches the house on one side, will have a distinct advantage over a freestanding structure: Winds will be considerably less

Auditioning a Spot

Try this: Using a portable grill and a table and chairs, set up some torches to create a temporary outdoor space and see what it's like to cook and eat in that location. Note the path you most naturally take to the site, and mark it with powdered lime or a garden hose. See what it feels like to transport the makings of a meal as well as dishes, silverware, glassware, and beverages out to the spot and back into the house afterward. Realistically assess the site based on the effort expended to carry everything there, as well as your enjoyment of the site once seated and eating. Repeat this experiment as necessary until you have found the best spot for your needs.

ABOVE: Bringing indoor chairs outside is a great way to try out possible dining areas. Here, this picnic in sight of the bay uses food packed easily in a basket.

fierce, rain and snow may infiltrate less, and the wear of weather on the kitchen elements may be moderated.

On the other hand, an attached outdoor kitchen may not really feel like the outdoors, because it occupies a space so close to the house. Also, because of its proximity to the doors and windows of your home, it may require the installation of an exhaust fan to direct heat and smoke away from the building.

Finally, although it is always important to design your outdoor kitchen with the style of your home in mind, it is even more crucial when it is actually attached to the house. Keep the scale consistent, choose similar materials and style elements, and use the roofline of the house as your guide when designing a roof for the outdoor kitchen.

A freestanding outdoor kitchen

If you choose to build your kitchen away from the house, you'll have more leeway when it comes to layout, space, and the overall look. Your kitchen could be a partial freestanding structure—a roof on posts, or a pavilion with half-walls—offering a charming shelter while housing cooking elements. Or it could be built onto an existing boundary wall and protected by a shed roof, enticing you to the far end of your yard.

If you'd like an actual building, gazebos are a great option, as you can have them delivered already assembled or built on site, or build them yourself from kits or plans. They are available in wood or vinyl in a tremendous variety of sizes, shapes, and styles, and some manufacturers offer the

option of fitting them with screens and/or windows, which can extend your season of use. Alternatively, you can design (or have designed) a building that perfectly suits your site and your own style of outdoor cooking and entertaining.

Another option is an island without roof or walls. This will still function as a distinct destination and act as a magnet whenever you or your guests are outside. An island can be built of prefabricated cabinets or on-site out of bricks or concrete blocks covered in stucco, or be entirely finished and shipped to you by a specialty manufacturer.

One drawback of a freestanding outdoor kitchen is its vulnerability to weather, because it's not sheltered by the mass of your home. You'll also have farther to trek from your indoor kitchen, with the result that you may want to add major appliances like a refrigerator and cabinets for convenience. A location away from the house will also likely require more labor to run utilities, as well as for transporting building materials and built-in components if it's not easily accessed by truck. There are ways to cut the utility expense—you can install an outdoor kitchen island that just requires a propane tank—but most people will at least want a pedestal electric outlet to provide power for lights or that all-important blender.

Consider topography

If you are thinking about a steep location for your outdoor kitchen, you need to weigh the cost of building over the incline (in the case of a deck) versus bringing in heavy equipment to level the area.

TERRACES

If you choose to recontour the land, you will be moving earth, which may require the construction of retaining walls, which can be

Thanks to the symmetrical hip roof that covers both pool equipment and cooking area, this poolhouse outdoor kitchen looks like a square pavilion. It has two sheltered eating places—a dining bar under the roof and an umbrella table nearby.

made of stone, brick, interlocking concrete blocks, or treated wood such as railroad ties, to keep the levels stable and in place.

When planning such recontouring, consider how you will move from one level to another. Steps and grass or dirt ramps are possibilities, as well as paths. (Ramps are great if you'll be transporting supplies to your kitchen or dining area via wheeled cart, but steps can be more people-friendly because they are level and less slippery.) In

addition to steps, you'll need to connect the stairs to existing or new paths above and below the retaining walls/terraces to make a visible and functional route between all the areas of an outdoor series of rooms.

DECKS

Alternatively, it may make more sense to construct a deck over uneven ground. In this case, you need to decide on the relation of the deck to the ground: Will it be elevated, level with your indoor kitchen or living room door, or at ground level, with steps leading down to it? It could also be located partway between, with wide sitting landings. In siting your deck, consider the path of melting snow sliding off the roof, if you live in such a climate, as it can stress your finished structure and may require additional reinforcement.

If your deck is going to be elevated, think about how to treat the area beneath the deck, which has a tendency to become a

LEFT: Large riprap stones retain earth on this steep slope, interplanted with bushes and mat-forming creeping plants. The masonry oven and gas grill are built into the slope, making them seem like part of the landscape, an excellent example of working with, not against, a difficult site.

BELOW: Built above a slope in southern California, this generous deck features a sitting and plant ledge, an overhead trellis for plants, and a privacy wall. The result is an intimate, indoor room–like experience with the scenic benefits of the outdoors.

"no man's land" of random storage. If that space receives some light, you might be able to plant it with shade-loving ground-cover plants, or you could mount trellising between the supports and create a living screen of flowering vines and climbers (see p. 199 for more specific ideas on vertical plantings).

If your deck base gets little light, your choices are more limited. Many people cover the area with sheets of manufactured lattice and call it finished. However, you could put mirrors behind some of the lattice to add dimension when looking back at the house from the yard. You could also build a more interesting and dimensional lattice than the shallow mass-produced kind. Another option is to pierce the underdeck area selectively, with a mix of lattice in one area and columns or round moon windows in another. Finally, some manufacturers offer an under-the-deck ceiling and wall screen system that can turn that ground-level area into a sheltered screen porch. That means you could grill on the deck above, then eat down below in bug-free comfort, avoiding smoke and mess from the grill.

How to Recognize a Great Outdoor Kitchen Location

- Level ground
- Not too far from existing utilities
- Big enough for your entertaining needs
- Offers privacy
- Has the exposure you prefer
- Is not in the center of the yard, but off to one side or tucked away
- Gives you a chance to improve a spot that needs attention
- Has a nice view (if you have an imperfect location with a fabulous vista, and you've got the budget to correct some of the shortcomings, the view can trump all other considerations.)

Making the choice

Budget will certainly play a role in selecting a location, but often your setting will dictate your choice by providing the perfect place against the house near the back door or out in the garden against the shelter of an old brick wall. Walk around your house, paying close attention to the possibilities. The odds are very good that the right location will present itself.

Putting It Down on Paper

Your next step is to describe your location as systematically as you can on paper in list or paragraph form. Go out and take some rough measurements. Note what you like currently about this space and what you'd like to get rid of (maybe a tree or shrub you can't stand, or a wayward boulder) or need to screen (Is it exposed to the road? Do you have an unobstructed view of your garbage cans or the power plant for your air conditioning?). Mark down existing landscape plantings you can use and design around, as well as any architectural features you need to repair or want to replace, such as a rotting deck or an unattractive walkway. If there is a path that connects the house to the outdoor kitchen, do you like its material and the way it links the two?

These features can have profound implications for your budget. Tree removal, earth moving, tearing down, and rebuilding will each be expenses to consider, as will the costs of constructing new areas of patio, deck, or path. Similarly, you'll need to consider the cost of new trees and plantings, as well as hardscape materials such as pavers, bricks, or stone.

You can start your kitchen plan by roughly sketching out the way your space looks now; this is a good way to make yourself pay attention to the details of your yard. It doesn't matter how well you draw—what's important is that you understand the specific benefits and challenges of the space you are considering.

Take photographs

Photograph your outdoor space, getting as clear a 360-degree orientation as you can manage. It's a curious fact that sometimes things show up better in photos than they do in actual 3D reality. Photographs also give you the opportunity to play with ideas over the course of weeks or months. If you're planning to put in an outdoor kitchen in the spring, take a slew of photos during the summer and/or fall so you can use them to plan over the winter months.

Take pictures in the morning, at midday, and in the early evening to see how sun and shade patterns track across your intended space. Look at how trees block the sun and where their shadows fall at different times of the day. See how the house itself creates a shadow and note the lines of that shadow at morning, noon, and dusk. These patterns will shift with the seasons, as the angle of the sun changes; if you have the luxury of time, make an effort to take pictures during the different seasons, particularly if you intend to get more than one season's use from your outdoor space. Also take pictures looking back at the house, as well as from the house toward the intended space to make sure you are happy with what you see.

Once you've got your photographs, you can either scan them or download them into your computer and try out different elements, using software such as Garden Designer or Home Architect® that allows you to insert your photos, as well as accurate dimensions, and will generate pictures and plans.

How to Measure and Draw a Site Map

Once you've settled on a location, you'll want to make a site map. Get a supply of graph paper divided into 1/4-in. squares, a tape measure, and a companion to hold the other end of the tape and help record measurements. This is going to take some time, so plan accordingly. You will be transferring measurements to the scale of 1/4 in. = 1 ft. You'll need powdered lime (available from garden stores) or outdoor marking paint (available at hardware or paint stores) for marking the boundaries of your kitchen on grass, or a garden hose or stakes and twine, along with rags or plastic tape to note the measuring points (or to make a grid).

Measure the length and width of the intended area and mark those edges with lime or paint or stakes and twine, or by outlining it with garden hose. Measure in from those landmarks (note the position from which you measure anything by using a rag or tape tied on the boundary line), noting the size and location of trees, bushes, big rocks, existing plantings, and so on, and transfer these locations and dimensions to your diagram. When you have completed the plan, also note places where the ground changes from level to high or low, so you know where the contours shift.

Once you've made a site map, make lots of copies. If you blow up or scale down the plan, make sure to keep track of the inch-to-foot scale, so that when you add elements, you can do so in proper proportion.

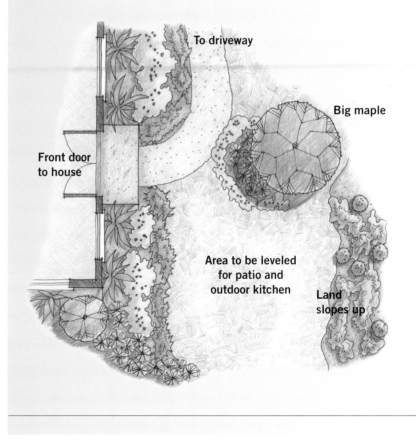

To driveway

Big maple

Front door to house

Area to be leveled for patio and outdoor kitchen

Land slopes up

Put your dream in the setting and see if it works

As you look at a particular location, consider the components you most want and where to place them. Perhaps you want a grape or wisteria-covered pergola for dining and a complete outdoor kitchen for cooking. For the benefit of the grapes or flowers, you'll want to locate the pergola in your sunniest spot. In contrast, you might want the kitchen area to be in light shade (unless you find that you only get out to the grill once the sun is low on the horizon) so that the cook is comfortable. Look at your photos with an eye to finding two adjacent spots, one sunny and the other less so. If you can't, you'll need to either adjust your plans (maybe separate the cooking and dining areas) or look for another place that does fulfill your requirements.

Your Outdoor Kitchen as a Room

Even though it's outside, think of the space where you'll be cooking as a room—if you do, you'll end up with a more functional design.

The ground beneath you

The "floor" of the outdoor kitchen can go a long way in establishing the overall feel of your kitchen—consider the difference between a patterned brick terrace, a natural stone patio with fragrant herbs growing in the spaces in between, and a gray-stained wooden deck with white accents.

Whatever you choose, remember to plan for drainage and to run any utilities you may need now or in the future under the floor area. After that, although the degree of ground preparation will differ by climate, all floor areas will require some amount of preliminary work before a finished floor is laid down.

CONCRETE

Concrete can be poured, scored, and/or colored to look like stone or tile. Precast concrete pavers, which can be laid down to form a floor, are widely available in a variety of sizes and can look like brick, flagstone, cobblestone, or just about any natural material. These range in size from small to large and can be found in home centers, landscape yards and nurseries, and online. Pavers or a poured floor must be set on a level bed of sand; in cold climates they may require footings and (if installed poorly) may be vulnerable to freezing and thawing cycles.

CERAMIC AND BRICK

Ceramic tile floors are especially suitable for warm climates and can be found in a wide and wonderful variety of shapes, sizes, and colors. Some are made to look like bricks or pavers, whereas others mimic stone at a fraction of the price. Because brick and low-fired ceramic floors are relatively soft and porous, they are unsuitable for cold climates unless protected by a roof or set in

such a way that they do not freeze and thaw with standing water on them. Stoneware tiles are stronger because they are fired at a higher temperature, but are still susceptible to freezing water.

Bricks can be set in decorative patterns (as can concrete pavers that imitate brick or stone); they can be interplanted with creeping aromatic herbs if they are not mortared in place, and, with a little encouragement, can grow mosses and very rapidly look like they're ages old. Whether you are using bricks or tiles, they will need to be set on a level area on top of several inches of sand poured over gravel, or installed over a concrete base.

STONE

Stone pavers, flagstone, bluestone, slate, and more are available as evenly thick, straight-edge cut tiles, or as "landscape stone," irregularly shaped pieces of relatively even and flat stone. Landscape stone is the less expensive choice of the two and often comes on a pallet in lots of 100 sq. ft. or more. Both kinds of stone require a flat area of sand and gravel to rest on. They can be ce-mented in place or laid without mortar.

Gravel is an even less expensive alternative and is particularly effective when combined with other materials, such as a checkerboard of flagstones and gravel, or used as filler between concrete pavers. If gravel is used as the sole flooring material, it will need to be raked regularly to keep it level.

GRASS OR BEATEN EARTH

Grass or clover can be a wonderful carpet in an outdoor kitchen without a roof—it's soft underfoot and easily mown. Beaten earth is an effective and time-honored solid floor in dry climates and can be swept regularly to keep the dust down.

DECKING

Your choices are wood (pressure-treated yellow pine, redwood, cedar, ipe, locust, teak), wood and plastic composites, or entirely plastic decking materials. Each offers advantages and comes with drawbacks. You may love the look and feel of natural wood, but dislike having to maintain it. Composite and plastic decking are easy to clean, don't require annual upkeep, and are green build-

RIGHT: Cast cement elements infilled with gravel and separated by strips of grass make a dramatic outdoor floor in southern California.

ing materials, but may not appeal to you. There's also the question of price: Decking is priced by the linear foot and prices can vary enormously from material to material. In making your decision, consider the life span and maintenance requirements of the decking you're thinking about.

Any deck you choose to build will require some kind of a base, such as concrete block or footings, depending on the climate. Decks are usually covered by local building codes (you or your contractor will need to get a permit) and there may be specific requirements for the type of foundation needed, as well as a determination as to whether or not railings and/or handrails are needed and what the stair dimensions should be. If any electrical, natural-gas, or water lines need to be run, you'll again need to comply with code. If your intended deck is near your property line, be aware of any

setback requirements. If you live in a community where there is a convenant, check that your design fits in with local requirements. Finally, if you want a heavy piece of equipment such as a big gas grill on your deck, be sure it is built to adequately support the weight.

The walls around us

Your outdoor kitchen can have actual walls, either halfway up to a roof or all the way, or it can have "walls" that are suggestions of boundaries, made by planting hedges, building stone walls, setting a row of plants in pots along the perimeter, or constructing raised beds to grow vegetables, flowers, or herbs. In this sense, a wall is anything that defines the outer edge of the kitchen area and can include things like torches set at the corners of the outdoor kitchen/dining area or lattice mounted

between corner posts. However achieved, it is important to have "walls" of some kind to mark the edges of the space and to announce the transition from "inside" the outdoor kitchen to the yard.

There are a number of materials and strategies for making "walls."

BUILT WALLS

Posts: These can range from fence posts planted in the earth to 6×6 beams mounted on concrete foundations. They can be freestanding or support a solid or fabric roof or trellises along the top or sides of the "room."

Half-walls: Half-walls go from ground level up to about countertop level, or a bit higher to create a wide shelf for a sitting bar, if desired. They can be made of siding materials or formed from the backs of outdoor cabinets or equipment. In many climates, half-walls can be made of concrete blocks covered with stucco, or adobe bricks, or by straw bale construction, as well as brick, stone, or wood.

Screen walls: Insect screening can be used to make walls, either by creating permanent screen walls or through the use of pull-down screens. Other types include hurri-

cane screens made of metal, as well as the retractable metal screens more often used to protect store windows.

Lattice: Pierced wood or intersecting slats of wood can be used to make decorative screens that offer privacy and plant supports. They make wonderful outdoor walls because they are somewhat open and yet define an edge. For durability, choose wood that has been treated for outdoor use.

Wooden fences: Stock fencing materials can be used to create walls in an outdoor kitchen, whether it is a closed (like a stockade fence) or open design (a picket fence). Like other wall materials, they can extend to the full height of the "wall" or be set at half-wall level.

PLANTED WALLS

Hedges: Hedging plants such as boxwood or other dense shrubs can create an extraordinary series of "walls" around an outdoor kitchen. They can be kept trimmed to function as half-walls or be allowed to grow to full height. Best of all, windows and doors can be cut into such hedges, creating magical, growing rooms.

ABOVE: A palapa, or thatched grass roof, creates a boldly textured shelter for this rustic outdoor kitchen made of peeled logs.

LEFT: Wisteria creates a side wall and ceiling over this pergola.

FACING PAGE: This white-painted custom-built lattice almost feels like a solid wall because it provides such a strong sense of separation from the rest of the garden.

A Little Bake House in the Woods

An alternative to creating the sense of a room outdoors is to actually build one. Cookbook author and baker Fran Gage built herself a freestanding kitchen among the giant redwoods in her backyard. Designed for serious patisserie and bread making, it's also used for entertaining family and friends.

ABOVE: A beehive-shaped masonry oven takes pride of place. The countertop and floor are concrete and there's plenty of space for storage. A fold-out table allows for entertaining.

LEFT: At night, the bake house glows like a lantern in a small clearing between the trees. The hipped roof is metal, and has a cupola at its peak, which helps heat escape.

Vines: Vines such as wisteria, grape, or kiwi can be grown over metal or wooden frameworks to create outdoor rooms. These can be planted to form walls, ceilings, or both, and offer an opportunity for flowers and fruits that enhance the entire outdoor experience.

Borders and/or raised beds: A flower border can provide a space with a growing, blooming edge. This can also be accomplished with long planters or raised beds.

Plants in pots: Arranged in a row, large flowering plants in big pots make a statement along an edge and offer a chance to have growing things closer to table or counter level.

Topping it off

A roof made of cedar shakes, slate, asphalt roofing tile, curved terra-cotta tiles, metal roofing, or even tarpaper will offer you, your guests, and your equipment protection from the weather, especially if a deep roof overhang further protects the interior. Other possible roof materials include thatch, called palapa, and palm roofs, both of which are available nationally from Internet sources. Consider adding a cupola at the peak, as this functions as a heat chimney to exhaust hot air, smoke, and grease.

A canvas fly or tarpaulin will keep out rain and provide shade. There are other options that provide less protection but make up for it in charm: a pergola covered with grapes or wisteria, for example. Inexpensive sheet lattice can also be used to build a shelter, mounted on posts and beams for walls and/or a ceiling. Wire strung with glass or paper tea-light lanterns, perhaps mounted from the house on one side and a boundary fence on the other, makes for a party atmosphere and a "ceiling" against the night sky.

Kitchen Geography: The Layout of Your Outdoor Kitchen

As a kitchen designer, I typically spend the bulk of my time with a client figuring out the kitchen's geography, or where to locate the major appliances and their associated storage. This is equally important in an outdoor cooking area if it is a full kitchen where food preparation is taking place. It is much less important, however, if you'll only be cooking food that was prepped inside.

Just as you would in an indoor kitchen, give each appliance and task as much room as possible on both sides. This allows more than one cook to work at a time. If the grill is set in one run of counters, a sink and refrigerator in another, and perhaps a wood-fired oven along a third leg, there's always going to be plenty of room to prepare, cook, and plate food. But even if your outdoor kitchen is a one-grill station, you will still be well served by including a dedicated prep and serve place, such as a worktable.

Even the simplest kitchen requires several important elements: a place to cook, a place to set food down going on or coming off the grill, and a place to eat and socialize. Also useful are places to store fuel and weatherproof covers for the grill and table; outdoor dishes and glassware, if kept outside; and tablecloths, napkins, candles, bug spray, and chair pads. If you use candles, hurricane shades, kerosene lanterns, or other portable light fixtures, they need to be stored away when not in use.

If your proposed kitchen is more elaborate, with a sink, refrigerator, wood-fired oven, and grill with side burners, you will have to plan even more carefully for utilities as well as efficient and functional space allocation. In my indoor kitchen design work, I divide every kitchen into four zones: hot, cold, wet, and dry. The first three are each anchored by a major appliance and each needs to have storage for associated tools and supplies.

Built in one line against a cement wall, this outdoor kitchen is a good example of how to use the borders of a space. Because it's a one-line arrangement, there's nothing separating the cook from guests, so they can pitch in at will.

In this unusual open triangle kitchen arrangement, the dining bar is far enough away from the gas grill to protect guests from smoke and grease.

The hot zone: The hot area (grill, smoker, wood-fired oven) needs space for fuel, barbecue and oven tools (pizza peels, tongs, iron push bars, etc.), pot holders and mitts, aprons, pans for the oven or for use on a side burner, wood chips for smoking, and so on. You'll also need 3 ft. to 4 ft. of heat-proof counter area in this zone, either on both sides of the grill or on an island that parallels the grill or wood oven (or both).

For built-in grills using bottled gas, your grill cabinet will need a cavity to store the gas cylinder. If you use a natural-gas hookup, you'll need to route the gas line to the connection point. (Be sure to order the appropriate connection for natural gas or LP grill, as the fixture for each is different.) If your grill is electric, you'll need an appropriate power connection, either 220v or 110v, depending on the grill. If you use charcoal or wood pellets, plan a storage area that keeps the damp out, such as a tightly covered can hidden in a base cabinet.

The cold zone: This refers to the refrigerator and icemaker, plus space for moving food in and out of the fridge, even if it's the counter area above a small undercounter cooler. If you make drinks, use a blender or juicer, or store and serve lots of soda or lemonade, give yourself as much space as possible to perform those tasks, and don't forget to plan for electrical outlets.

The wet zone: The wet zone is where the water is—the sink area (or hose). Just like indoors, you'll need waterproof (and weatherproof) counter space by the sink for dirty things on one side and clean on the other, even if you are only washing vegetables. Figure a minimum of 2 ft. to 3 ft. on each side, if possible, for maximum functionality, and leave some storage space for colanders, vegetable brushes, and other tools you'll use in this area.

The dry zone: This is the only area that lacks an appliance, but it's still important because food preparation, serving, and plating take place here. Even if your outdoor kitchen only consists of a grill, you need a dry zone to put down platters. It should be heatproof, easy to sanitize, and impervious to weather. A zinc- or stainless steel–topped table with a shelf underneath is a simple and functional example; a built-in island covered in stucco and tile is more elaborate. A 3-ft.-long dry zone is recommended; a 5-ft. or longer area is even better.

Putting it together

Just like the kitchen inside the house, your outdoor kitchen should fit the way you cook and the people who cook with you. A lone chef will need a small and efficient space to move between the grill and the preparation area, whereas multiple cooks will each want enough space to work without bumping elbows with the others. If many people cook at once in an outdoor kitchen with lots of equipment, plan space

Kitchen Geometry: Pick the Setup that Works Best for You

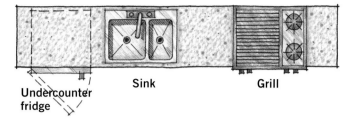

Undercounter fridge **Sink** **Grill**

1. One long line: This arrangement is the simplest to build, as there are no dead corners. Its openness invites participation.

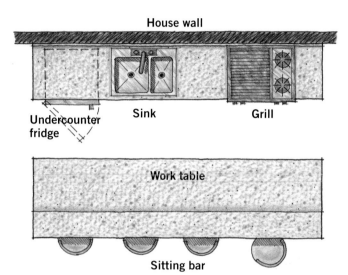

House wall

Undercounter fridge **Sink** **Grill**

Work table

Sitting bar

2. Two parallel lines: This has the virtue of simplicity; the addition of an island adds dining-bar space as well as a barrier that differentiates the cooking area from the guests.

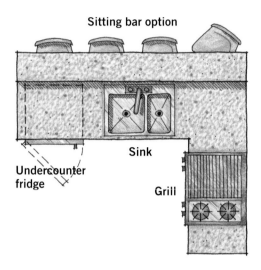

Sitting bar option

Undercounter fridge **Sink** **Grill**

3. Ell-shaped: This arrangement can invite or separate, depending on its orientation to the rest of the yard. Because there are two distinct areas, it's a very comfortable arrangement for two cooks.

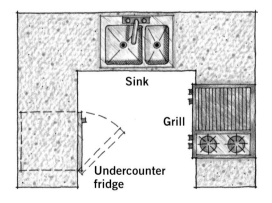

Sink **Grill** **Undercounter fridge**

4. U-shaped: This kitchen offers lots of preparation space and the chance to incorporate multiple appliances.

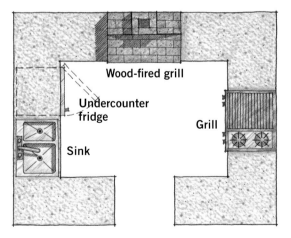

Wood-fired grill **Undercounter fridge** **Grill** **Sink**

5. Square: This outdoor kitchen allows a leg for each zone, giving the maximum amount of counter space between each area. Because it's enclosed, it doesn't invite others to cook with you, but it does offer lots of spots for dining bars.

Prevailing Winds

Unfortunately, winds shift, often frequently. Nevertheless, there are prevailing winds that determine the direction of smoke, at least some of the time. Wheel your portable grill to your proposed site, spend several evenings there cooking and dining, and you'll discover the prevailing wind. (It's better to do this with a grill than a candle or incense stick, because the amount of smoke is much more visible and because you'll be there longer.)

for each cook and appliance by giving each zone its own run of counter to create "stations." There are lots of possible layouts; perhaps one of these will best suit your situation:

One long line: Cabinets can be installed side by side to form a freestanding island, or can be set against the back of the house to create an efficient outdoor kitchen. If you are using all possible appliances, follow the usual progression of food, moving ingredients from the refrigerator, to the sink, then to the grill, and finally the counter for serving, from left to right.

Two parallel lines: An island that parallels one long run of counters is an extremely functional layout both outside and inside, particularly if it has no appliances on it. Make the island a dedicated food preparation and plating zone, put seating on the far side of it, if you wish, and glory in the open space.

Ell-shaped: A kitchen shaped in an ell will easily allow more than one person to cook at the same time, as each chef can be working on a different leg. Spread out the zones and appliances so the grill is on a different leg than the sink and refrigerator, and give each ell enough counter space to be really useful (a continuous 3 ft. or more). You can also add an island for even more functionality.

U-shaped: This configuration welcomes guest chefs, as there are three different zones to work at. You might want to put a sink on one leg, a refrigerator on another, and a grill on the third, or perhaps keep the fridge and sink together and have a counter completely dedicated to food preparation and serving. A U-shaped kitchen can be further customized with the addition of an island or central worktable, which will provide even more workspace.

Square: An outdoor kitchen that uses all four legs of a square will tend to be a one-person kitchen unless it's built on a grand scale. That's because once you get trapped inside the square it's not so easy to exit. On the other hand, a square allows you to make each run of counter a separate and dedicated zone, while also providing room for hot-zone extras like a wood-fired oven or smoker.

Cook where you eat? Eat where you cook?

It's best to locate the cooking area at the edge of the social space, in a kind of sheltered alcove created by planting or screening, or alongside of your home, the garage, or an outbuilding. Allow plenty of space for the cook and for friends—for instance, a dining bar offers all of the pleasures of an eat-in kitchen island, giving both the cook and guests a chance to talk while cooking is in progress. However, a shift in the wind can change all of that. In my ideal outdoor world, you'd have a great place to socialize while cooking, but you'd also have another dedicated dining area that's far enough away from the grill to protect you from smoke, grease, and excess heat.

Whether adjacent or separate, it's a good design idea to visually differentiate the cooking space from the social space. One

way to do this is to plan the cooking area as a functional, efficient space, in contrast to a more relaxed décor in the social space. The cooking area could be constructed of stone and stainless steel, whereas the dining area might be centered on a long wooden table draped with a patterned cloth, illuminated by candlelit lanterns, and surrounded by large pots of fragrant, night-blooming flowers. See Chapter 4 for a fuller treatment of the dining and entertaining area.

Kitchen Style: Integrating Indoor and Outdoor Design

An outdoor space does not exist in a vacuum, and works best if it relates back to the shape of your yard or garden and your home. Landscape designer Gordon Hayward has written a useful book, *Your House/Your Garden* (W. W. Norton, 2003), in which he

urges readers to design their gardens in close relation to their houses. This means mirroring the scale of your indoor rooms out of doors and having garden paths that are extensions of your doorways and halls.

For instance, if your kitchen is 12 ft. square and you're building an outdoor kitchen just beyond the French doors in your kitchen, you could construct a stone patio area that reflects the 12-ft. square. If the outdoor space is a distance beyond the door, construct a path in line with (and in proportion to) the door, so there is a natural flow between the outdoors and indoors.

Think too about matching the style of your outdoor space with that of your home. Whether you live in a Georgian-style home or a Levitt® house, your outdoor kitchen should reflect and relate back in terms of style, proportion, scale, design, and

Making a Preliminary Outdoor Kitchen Design Plan

At this point you should have lots of ideas for equipment, layouts, paths, and amenities, well-filled files, and an accurate scale drawing of your outdoor space, either drawn by hand or by computer. Get a pad or roll of tracing paper and art masking tape (it comes away easily without tearing paper). Lay the tracing paper over your site map and locate the elements of your outdoor kitchen. The existing landscape features should already be on the scale drawing and the elements you put in now would include the possible paths, appliances, counters, and other built portions of the plan, such as the patio or deck area(s). Also indicate new areas of planting and other features. Be careful to keep the scale consistent at 1/4 in. = 1 ft.

You can repeat this as you go through the book, and through the design process, using pencil and eraser to modify the plan. You can also use multiple pieces of tracing paper to try out lots of different layout ideas. Copy the tracing-paper plans onto white paper on a copy machine to use as a base for further tracing-paper changes, or to add color with ink or paint.

Don't forget your utilities: Add an overlay to show the location of present electric, gas, or water lines, whether you'll be wanting those in your outdoor kitchen or not. The last thing you want later on is a backhoe ripping into a gas line you didn't know was there. If you don't know where or whether these utilities run through your yard, call your local utility offices and town manager. This information should be automatically triggered by the permit process, but if it isn't, know that every state has rules and laws that pertain to excavation and utilities. Call the national referral number (888-258-0808) to get the number of your local One-Call Center to find out about excavation issues in your area.

If you want to add any of these utilities to your outdoor kitchen space, show how and where they'll be routed in. Also mark drainage routes and sites, both for water you may bring or pipe in and for rainfall and runoff. If you plan on electric lighting, you will use this drawing later on to make a light map.

The accuracy of the original scale drawing is crucial to the success of the whole design. If you have doubts about your ability to execute an accurate scale drawing, hire a professional to do it for you.

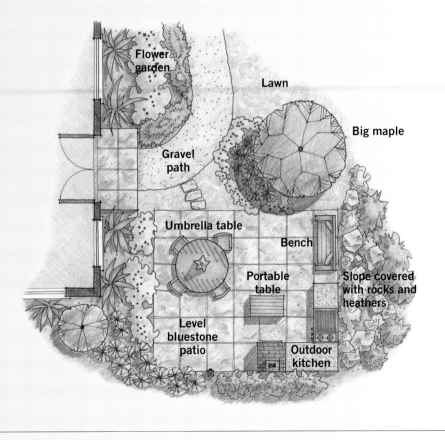

RIGHT: Common bricks are used here to make a path wide enough for two to walk side by side. The alternating pattern adds visual interest.

BELOW: Built up with layers of compacted earth, the path's surface is dressed with gravel, its edges marked with stone; larger stones have been used to construct the risers of steps.

materials. For example, a brick house would suggest a brick-walled outdoor kitchen or a custom grill built of brick. For a clapboard farmhouse in a rural setting, define the space with plantings and stone walls or wooden fences, with a stone patio. A California bungalow covered in stucco would demand a stucco-covered kitchen island, perhaps partially sheltered by a terra-cotta tiled roof.

Filling Out Your Plan

Use landscape elements to enhance your plan—create raised beds to make a border around the patio, or bring in trees and shrubs to provide shade, serve as wind breaks, or add blooms and/or fragrance. Consider other vertical accents, such as topiaries, tuteurs, or posts planted with vines, as well as water features large and small. For a more detailed discussion of landscaping, see pp. 193–201. For now, simply consider planted elements you might want as you design the kitchen, leaving room for them on your plan.

Paths

Once you've found the natural path to your site (see "Auditioning a Spot" on p. 9), think how to make that route more interesting. If it's a straight line, can it take a gentle curve without looking contrived? Could the curve wrap around a garden area, large container planting, or water feature? A good way to try out possible paths is by laying garden hose along the route on the ground. If you use two parallel lengths of hose, you can experiment with the width of the path. The width will determine whether people walk in single file (32 in. yields a narrow, one-person path that is still wheelchair accessible) or side by side (45 in. to 60 in.). Although a wider path has a more gracious feel to it, you probably don't want to make boulevards in your backyard unless your property and your kitchen are on a grand scale. You can also make a path flow from narrow to wide and back again, much like a landing on a stair. See if you can add a bench to create a social place as you move through the yard, or put a fountain on one side of the path to add sensual delight. Don't forget to plan for path lights—they're essential to make evening navigation easy and safe (see p. 185 for more on the subject).

PATH MATERIALS

You have many options, from mowing a path through a meadow to wood mulch, gravel, stepping-stones, flagstones, cultured stone paving, concrete, brick, or tile. If you are going to be transporting food and such on wheels, construct a path that's as smooth as possible, using beaten earth, flagstones, or poured concrete. Soft paths need regular upkeep. A grass path requires mowing, a dirt path needs frequent traffic to keep weeds from getting the upper hand, and a mulch path must be replenished once every year or two, but all these options are inexpensive and a path constructed from them can often be finished in a matter of hours. A good idea is to start with a soft path and change over to something more permanent later on if you wish.

Hard materials require more prep work. The ground must be leveled, a layer of sand or gravel or both must be installed for drainage, concrete may be required for some materials, and, in cold climates, a deeper foundation of some sort will be necessary. Note that even if you are installing stepping-stones, although you don't need to level the entire area, you do need to dig them in and make them level with the surrounding dirt. Although such paths can be installed by homeowners, many prefer to hire profes-

Have You Covered Everything? Checking Your Design Plan

- How have you defined the edges of the kitchen and/or dining areas?
- What will the "floor" of the kitchen be: grass, stone, concrete, pavers, wooden decking, brick?
- Have you provided overhead protection for the eating area and/or cooking area?
- Have you planned for a gas line now or at a later date?
- Is there enough light to cook and clean up effectively? Is there adequate light in the eating/entertainment area?
- Is the route to the kitchen easy to navigate and well lit? Is the same true of the path from the cooking area to the eating area, if they are separated?
- Have you marked electrical connections and routes on your plan, including those already existing and those to be added?
- Have you planned for enough outlets to run everything from a blender to a fountain to party lights?
- Have you planned for overhead fans?
- Do you want to include a heater or live fire element for extending the season?
- If you want an outdoor sink, have you planned for the source of water (from a hose, or will you need to run pipe)? Have you accounted for drainage?
- In climates where water can freeze, have you made provisions for draining any pipes at the end of the season?
- Are the smoke-producing appliances sited to take advantage of prevailing breezes? As much as possible, have you sited them away from seating?
- How is the outdoor kitchen equipment protected from weather?
- Have you made sure there is enough space around the table and chairs to walk by easily?
- Is there enough storage for everything you want to store outside, from grilling equipment to pillows for the furniture to fuel for the fire?
- Do you need storage for the outdoor furniture itself out of season? Or have you planned for covers?
- Do you know where you'll keep garbage?
- Do you know what, if anything, you may want to add in the future, and have you planned adequately for those future requirements? Most especially, have you planned for utilities and anything else that requires digging?
- Have you made your kitchen as beautiful as it can be?

sional help such as masons or landscapers for all but stepping-stones or gravel paths, as permanent paths need tamping or heavy compacting and require lots of weighty materials to be brought to the site and leveled.

As a result, most permanent paths are pricey but, once paid for, require little upkeep. (Gravel, the easiest of such paths to install, will need regular weeding and replenishing at intervals of several years, as well as annual raking.)

Who You Gonna Call?
Bringing in the Professionals

If you are considering a kitchen of some size or complexity, or if the surrounding landscape needs a lot of work, I suggest you begin with a landscape architect or garden designer to review how the kitchen is going to sit within your home landscape. Contractors who specialize in outdoor kitchen con-

struction routinely refer clients to landscape designers as a first step because there's no point in planning a kitchen until landscape plans are in place, along with utility routes and planning permissions (you or your building professional will need to submit a copy of the plan to get building permits). Often such professionals can make suggestions that will save you money. Discuss their fees (they may work on an hourly basis or quote you a flat fee for design work) and decide if you want them to make off-the-cuff suggestions or to create a detailed drawn-to-scale plan, complete with planting suggestions and placement. If you have made a design plan yourself, they can critique it and make suggestions. A landscape professional or garden designer will want to see the site for themselves and will expect you to have some sense of what you want in terms of appearance, as well as where you want to place your outdoor rooms. Some landscape professionals install hardscapes and gardens as well as design them, whereas others may design them but leave all or part of the installation to a contractor or landscaper.

With a landscape plan in hand, you can consult an architect on any custom-built elements, such as a deck, porch, pergola, or pavilion. The architect will create drawn or computer-generated plans that will include a bird's-eye view, an elevation (which shows how it will look from ground level), and construction details. The kinds of small projects that comprise garden buildings are generally inexpensive in terms of an architect's time. Expect the fee to be in the neighborhood of several thousand dollars for a complex deck or small building. Alternatively, if you want a small building that's fairly conventional, you can save a great deal of money by ordering a prefab structure, bypassing an architect altogether.

Once you've got your site plan and design finalized, it's time to get the work done. You've got several options.

Design/build firms do everything, designing, building, and installing a project for one set price. Increasingly, there are design/build firms that specialize in outdoor kitchens, often working in tandem or consultation with a landscaper. The advantage of such a firm is that you can get a contract price for the whole job, knowing they have the expertise to deal with the problems and surprises specific to outdoor kitchens.

You can hire a general contractor to do all the work after you've finalized your plan, or you can develop a plan in concert with a contractor. A contractor is responsible for getting permits (though you need to make sure this has been done). Some regions will have zoning and code requirements and the contractor should alert you to these, although they should also be triggered by the permitting process. The contractor will purchase materials and schedule deliveries, and plan for construction and installation of all the different elements of the project. The actual kitchen components are built by the contractor—he builds any structures, like the deck and/or patio (or coordinates building the patio if a landscaper does that portion). He builds the outdoor kitchen cabinets (if site built) or installs manufactured cabinets. He installs the appliances and coordinates the electrical and plumbing professionals. Note that all equipment comes with safe installation instructions, and most built-in gas grills, for example, are available in insulated versions (for installation into combustible surrounds such as wood) or uninsulated versions (for noncombustible surrounds such as stone). As you solicit bids and interview contractors, ask them how much experience they have in building outdoor kitchens.

An outdoor kitchen specialist is a contractor who has installed a number of outdoor kitchens and has chosen to specialize

Sharing Your Dream Files

Show your files to the professionals you decide to work with to give them a good sense of what you want. It's useful to see what a client has in mind, as descriptions are often less informative than a picture. The files are an invaluable guide to your sense of style and preferred ambiance, and present a visual portrait of your preferences.

in their construction. As a result, he may be more fluent in the kinds of problems (and their solutions) that are inherent in such projects. One way to find such specialists is to ask your patio and hearth retailer for recommendations. Consult friends, equipment dealers, the Yellow Pages, websites, etc. to find a local person who is equipped to do the work you need and who can provide good references.

Be aware that good contractors are often booked as much as a year in advance, so you may have to get in line. Also, contractors often will only do jobs of a certain scale—if your job isn't large enough, you'll need to find someone who takes small jobs or is less well known or less experienced.

A contractor can be an individual who works with one or two people and does mostly carpentry, or a general contractor can run a larger crew with masons, electricians, plumbers, painters, and carpenters. The person you hire can tell you if he is subbing out parts of the job or if he has the capacity (and licenses) to cover all the bases himself. When you hire a contractor, you may have the choice of paying for time and materials plus a set markup, or your building professional may offer you a set contract price that has his profit built into it. At the start of a project, the contract price will be higher. This, however, may not be the case by the end, as unforeseen events (such as hitting a rock ledge, for example) can considerably increase your final labor costs if you are paying by the hour instead of a set price. However, even a contract price arrangement will have clauses that allow for price increases should you change the design, or to allow for unexpected delays or discoveries.

Be sure to go over all the elements of the design with your contractor to make sure you are in agreement as to what is being done. Sometimes a contractor may want to modify the design for aesthetic or functional reasons, or to save you money. Carefully consider these suggestions and go back to the designer and/or architect if necessary to make an informed decision. Be very clear about noting any changes and make sure the contractor is ready to take responsibility for those changes by guaranteeing that the change will work or that he will fix it if it doesn't, particularly if the change is structural. Get all changes on paper, signed by both of you, to insure clear communication and to document your agreement.

Being Your Own General Contractor

Another option is to be your own project manager, hiring professionals as you need them. If you go this route, you are trading money for time, as you are the one responsible for coordinating all of the tradesmen and materials throughout the project. You must shepherd permits through the system, make sure the load of gravel comes when it's needed, and chase down the plumber to install the sink and faucet on time. You also choose each professional, trusting each of them to do their job on schedule and to your standard, and you will be paying them on an hourly basis (so if the gravel is late, you'll be paying the landscape crew to stand around and wait, for example).

The advantage is that you are in control of the project and can follow costs closely. Don't go this route unless you are detail-oriented, prepared to make this a close-to-full-time job, and ready to be informed and focused on all the tasks that need to be done. Having said that, it can be extremely rewarding both financially and emotionally to be your own general contractor. It also allows you to take on some of the jobs yourself, such as painting or planting, which can further save you money.

Before any of this
stonework was started,
a natural-gas line was
run underground to the
grill site.

The contractor should provide you with
a list of materials and their cost, and the
estimated cost of labor. You should have
by now researched the costs of appliances,
plant material, and installation labor, and
by adding all of these elements together, you
will have the approximate cost of construction. Many people suggest that you add 10
to 20 percent of this number as a cushion
to cover unexpected additions, changes, or
price increases.

If you have a big enough job and a list of
recommended contractors, put your project
out for bids and assess the differences in the
prices that come back. Make sure that you
are comparing apples with apples and try
to determine what makes one price higher
or lower than another. Be sure to ask for

references, specifically for outdoor kitchen
projects if they've done them, and don't be
shy about calling homeowners. Ask about
their insurance (and check your own policy
as well) and contact the Better Business
Bureau to make sure there are no com-
plaints on file about them. Be an informed
and responsible consumer and choose your
contractor carefully—you're going to have
a close relationship for a time and it's much
easier if you can trust your contractor to be
committed to bringing your plan to completion as designed.

It also makes a big difference if you can
check on your job in progress at least once a
day. If you're there when questions come up,
you'll be in a much better position to avoid
mistakes or to make sure they are rectified

promptly. This is true even if your contractor is working from detailed blueprints, so stay informed and available to get the result you're paying for.

The Budget Test

The expense of an outdoor kitchen rests on a number of factors, including the permanence of the construction, the materials and equipment you choose and the cost of installing them, and the complexity and scale of the final design. If you have to hire earthmovers to truck in fill, lay base coats of gravel and sand, and then lay stone slabs or pavers, you'll have a lot of money invested in the site long before you buy the first table, chair, grill, or electric fixture. Know what things cost before finalizing a design plan and make your choices accordingly.

Ask yourself: How much can I afford? How do I want to spend it? What's most important to me? These are crucial questions and must be answered honestly. As a designer, I've had the experience of being given a budget by a client and, after creating a design based on it, being informed that they are actually willing to spend much more to get their dream kitchen built.

From the other side, as a consumer, I've had my budget ideas laughed out of the park by building professionals who assume that a client's budget is either elastic or fiction. I believe it is very important to be truthful about your budget and realistic about what it can buy.

For example, if you have a sum of money set aside for an outdoor kitchen, do you want to put the bulk of it into the setting (a patio, pavilion, or deck) or into the equipment? Not everyone can afford to do both at once. My advice would be to put the money into the setting if you are planning

to stay at that location for a long time, and start with modest equipment that you can upgrade over time. If you think you'll be moving, buy the equipment of your dreams in portable form, so you can take it with you to the next house.

It doesn't all have to be done at once

Even though it is satisfying to complete a project all at once, it often makes good sense to plan a project in stages. Here's a progression that might make sense for many: Year One, bring in and bury the electrical, natural-gas, and/or water lines, construct a flagstone patio, and furnish it with a worktable, dining set, and a portable or built-in grill. Year Two could feature the installation of a sink and counters around the grill. Year Three might start with the construction of a pergola over the cooking area and the installation of a fan and outdoor lighting, and end with plants twining around the posts. In subsequent years you could upgrade equipment and/or furniture, do further landscaping, or build a wood-burning pizza oven.

If appropriate, create a series of plans that build on each other, perhaps labeled consecutively to denote that one or more years may pass between additions. Plan One might be what you'll do this year, whereas Plan Two may take another five years to realize, with Plan Three scheduled for a decade hence. By planning in stages and overlaying the plans on tracing paper, you can see how each plan morphs into its next incarnation over time.

Checking your dreams against an actual budget is the moment of truth; it can be hard if you find that the estimated cost of your kitchen is more than you budgeted. Remember you can build this outdoor dream in stages so that in the end you have the outdoor kitchen of your dreams.

Inexpensive and portable seating such as Adirondack chairs and a painted bench free up the budget for cooking equipment.

Artful Desert Living

Living for 18 years in the desert can be inspirational—at least it was for this Arizona family. They spent a good deal of time deciding how they wanted to use their land before embarking on landscaping and hardscaping. Because they host big parties several times a year, they planned their outdoor spaces to be both family- and entertaining-friendly, with a range of gathering places, both large and small. In addition to the outdoor kitchen, there's a dining

ABOVE: The floor is scored concrete with a perimeter rim of Castello stone, and the cooking wall is made of Kansas rubble stone. Stainless steel doors protect wood stored below the oven (right) and offer access to the gas cylinder (left). The serving platters on the mantle are from Tuscany.

LEFT: French park chairs and a long wooden table are set opposite the outdoor kitchen pavilion's wood-fired oven and gas grill. The roof is made of ceramic tile.

kitchen. The long kitchen table, which seats up to 10, can also be used for serving or setting up a buffet. This kitchen area is part of a U-shaped sequence of spaces that jut out on two sides from the back of the house. The portion that follows the lines of the house (and is just off the indoor kitchen) functions as a shallow shaded porch with seating. One projecting leg of the U is the outdoor kitchen and, opposite it, across a courtyard garden, is the living room area, which has a more intimate four-person dining area, as well as additional seating and a generous fireplace. Looking out from under the sheltering roof of any of these spots offers great desert views set off by the backdrop of distant mountains.

Moving farther away from the house, there are sunny patios, a pool area, and a thriving vegetable garden. In addition, there's a large grassy area designed to seat up to 18 guests, as well as a rose garden and cutting garden for the pleasure of friends and family.

ABOVE: Pull-out shelves behind the stainless steel doors make access easy.

RIGHT: Gratins baked in earthenware taste wonderful in a wood-fired oven.

FACING PAGE: The courtyard intersperses flagstone stepping-stones and grass to great effect. The galvanized steel sculptures are from a crafts market in Scottsdale.

room area, a gazebo, an upper living room with dining area, a sunset patio off the master bedroom, a desert walk with benches, and numerous other garden spots for relaxing and conversation. Because the couple are art collectors, they've furnished many of these outdoor spaces with sculptures that add unexpected touches of whimsy and delight.

The cooking area is devoted to high-heat cooking, with a wood-fired oven and a gas grill. There is no sink or refrigerator, because it's just a short walk from the indoor

LEFT: Even though the ingredients are French and Italian, the desert light is uniquely Southwestern.

BELOW: Comfortable seating is arranged in front of the fireplace on top of a sisal rug. The attractive cast aluminum furniture is light enough to move easily. A ceiling-mounted electric heater sends concentrated warmth down on chilly evenings when the fireplace alone is not enough. The floor is Castello Monasterere, arranged in an ashler pattern.

ABOVE LEFT: Set near the pool, large stones vary the terrain and inject a natural note. The steel sculpture is by local artist Gary Slater.

ABOVE RIGHT: Steps between the desert walk and the grassy entertainment area show the power of contrasting textures: Castello Monasterere travertine stone and lippia (a carpet grass) juxtapose hard and soft, smooth gray and green fluff.

LEFT: These whimsical stone sculpture chairs are surprisingly comfortable to sit on.

ABOVE: Poolside and adjacent to the outdoor kitchen, this glass-topped table and chairs cast vivid shadows in the desert light. The chairs originally belonged to the owner's grandmother, and were renewed with a fresh powder coating.

ABOVE RIGHT: From the front courtyard looking out to the street, double gates mark the public entrance to the property. Built on site by a local welder, their design is based on gates the owners saw in Italy and France.

RIGHT: At night the fireplace is a magnet, drawing everyone to the seating area under the porch's wooden roof. Small spotlights mounted on the ceiling illuminate the conversation area and decorative elements.

ABOVE: In the vegetable garden, raised beds are made of the same Kansas stone used elsewhere on the property. A metal framework overhead holds bamboo poles to shield the plants from the pounding desert sun.

RIGHT: California sculptor Larry C. Shank made this extraordinary fountain. The owners bought it as a 25th anniversary present for themselves after seeing a similar one in Napa.

Home on the Range

When one of the present owners of this family place married her husband, she also married into a large clan with deep roots in California. In the 1960s, her parents-in-law purchased this Lake County ranch located about an hour and a half from San Francisco. The parents commissioned Cambridge-based architect Bob Luchetti to design a home that their seven children and their families could use. Their son was the contractor on the project. These days, it's home to as many as 40 family members on holidays like Thanksgiving, and is a much-loved gathering place for this far-flung family.

The ranch is used for raising beef cattle and ranges over 650 acres scattered with wide plains, a stream, and live oak trees, along with wildflowers and the kind of big sky you only

ABOVE: Here, locally raised tri-tip steaks and sweet potatoes grill in the sweet smoke of the wood fire. Tri-tip steaks are a regional California meat cut, carved from the loin of beef. They are marvelous for grilling, and are sliced against the grain.

TOP RIGHT: At dusk, the flames of the smaller wood-fired grill glow in the firebox. The draft, or air intake, is controlled by opening or closing the doors.

BOTTOM RIGHT: The masonry oven's metal hood funnels smoke away from the chef and up the chimney as bread toasts in the heat. Fresh rosemary sprigs add flavor and aroma.

FACING PAGE: At each end of the arbor is a bench. From this one, you can hear the brook burbling and enjoy iced tea sheltered in the shade from the heat of the day.

see in the West. A deck off the home's indoor dining room offers those big-sky views on the other side of the house from the outdoor kitchen.

When the family planned and built their outdoor kitchen, they knew it had to be grand enough for big gatherings. To that end, the arbor can accommodate as many as 75 people under its sheltering shade, its long granite table will seat 12, and the wood-fired barbecue alongside the arbor can cook up a whole lamb or pig with ease. Perpendicular to the arbor and slightly closer to the house, a wood-fired masonry oven and a smaller wood barbecue are used for more intimate meals. Each of these cookers can be fitted with a rotating spit. San Francisco chef Mark Franz's wood-fired cooking expertise informed the design of these cookers. The outdoor cooking areas face the indoor kitchen, which has two sets of doors out to the patio, making it very easy to bring food and place settings in and out.

The deck off the dining room offers sunset views and a chance to watch the cattle graze. It's a favorite site for before-dinner drinks and snacks.

Pool-House Kitchen

If you're planning on building a pool house, consider adding a kitchen to it, as this couple did. Because pool houses require a full complement of electric and water hookups, adding a small and economical kitchen to the interior is a relatively minor budget increase. That's because when you install an auxiliary kitchen inside a pool house you can use conventional indoor equipment and choose stock indoor-quality cabinetry, as this couple did. They also opened the pool-house interior up to the outdoors with expansive double glass doors that link the kitchen to the adjoining patio. They have all the benefits of an outdoor kitchen by using the freestanding grill dining area under the pergola to cook foods prepped in the pool-house kitchen.

ABOVE: Teak chaise longues with white cushions match the color scheme of the building, which is faced with teak-colored stone on two sides and white clapboard on the others.

FACING PAGE: You can see how well-conceived this indoor/outdoor connection is: The pool-house kitchen functions as a shaded food-preparation area open to the grill and dining area in good weather, yet can be closed and used as an interior kitchen when the weather is inhospitable. Outside, the shaped rafter tails and decorative corbels at the tops of the posts of the pergola add pleasing detail. Plantings make a living half-wall around two sides of this dining area.

Because it is completely protected from the weather, the kitchen uses regular indoor equipment, but because the linking double doors open wide to the patio, the kitchen can function for outdoor living. A grill on the edge of the patio provides outdoor cooking space as well.

The Fire Outside

FACING PAGE:
A masonry oven combined with a charcoal grill offers this couple an outdoor kitchen that is completely wood-based. It's set into an alcove on the property's perimeter wall.

*F*ood cooked outdoors tastes wonderful, and that's the biggest reason to have an outdoor kitchen. Add the age-old human fascination with fire and the pleasures of a natural, open environment, and you have a recipe for pure social enjoyment as well as great eating. The grill is at the heart of the outdoor kitchen, and this chapter offers a guide to grills of every size, every type (built-ins and freestanding), and every fuel—wood, pellets, or charcoal; liquid propane or natural gas; dual fuel; or electric. I'll also look at cooking with fire in forms other than the grill—smokers, smoker-grills, wood-fired ovens, and roasting boxes. "Social fire," such as fireplaces and fire pits, is covered in Chapter 4.

RIGHT: A freestanding grill can be wheeled wherever you want it, making an outdoor kitchen into a portable affair. Placed right outside, it's easy to bring out prepped food, then carry the cooked food back upstairs for a meal on the porch.

Grills

For many people, outdoor cooking is all about the grill. At its simplest, it's a cooking grate set over an intense heat source. Grills can be fueled by charcoal, natural gas or propane, wood pellets, or electricity, and are available in a variety of sizes and designs. You can buy freestanding grills (usually set on wheels) or "drop-in" configurations for permanent installation, and you can add side burners or an electric rotisserie to a basic setup. Whatever grill you choose, nearly all require protection from harsh weather, either a removable vinyl cover or a permanent design feature such as a built-on lid or a roof or awning high over the cooking area.

Why Does It Taste So Good? Flavor, Heat, and Food Chemistry

Food that is seared at a high temperature develops flavors that are just not possible on conventional indoor equipment. When food is exposed to high heat, a complex chemical reaction called the Maillard effect takes place. Carbohydrates combine with amino acids to produce hundreds of by-products, a dark color, and the wonderful combination of flavors and succulence that inspires outdoor cooking around the world.

This is only possible with relatively thin and even cuts of meat, poultry, fish, or vegetables. If you want to grill or high-heat roast larger, thicker cuts of meat or whole birds, they must be butterflied flat, cooked on a rotisserie, roasted on a can of beer or another kind of upright roaster with a liquid reservoir, or cooked indirectly over lower heat or with smoke (as in a smoker for true barbecue).

Cooking meats and vegetables together on skewers is another way to flash cook; even relatively thick chunks of meat grill fast when they're cut into cubes.

Pick your price, pick your grill

There's literally a grill to fit anybody's budget, with less expensive options in the two- and three-figure range and heavier, more elaborate grills available for thousands of dollars. At every level, however, charcoal grills are always less expensive than comparable gas grills, although there is still quite a price range within the charcoal category.

Typically, what separates a cheap grill from its more expensive cousins are its overall size and the size of the grill surface, the number of BTUs or degree of heat it puts out (this applies only to noncharcoal grills), the heaviness or gauge of the metal (and, in the case of gas, the grill burners), the quality of construction, and whether or not it offers extras such as electric or gas ignition, a rotisserie, or side burners.

The gauge of metal matters because thin sheet steel will dent and rust more easily than stronger, thicker steel. Heavier metals also offer some insulation protection, because a thin metal will conduct heat rapidly. Heavy cast stainless steel, cast iron, or cast brass burners will perform better over a longer time than thinner, flimsier models. All together, a weighty, well-made grill will last much longer than an inexpensive grill made of inferior materials.

What to look for when buying a grill or smoker

Whether you choose charcoal or gas (or wood pellets or electric), here are some general considerations to keep in mind.

Quality of construction: Does the grill or smoker seem solid or rickety? If you shake it gently, does it hold up or does it shimmy or, worse, rattle and squeak? Are the joints welded rather than being held together with screws or nuts and bolts? Are the corners square? Do the doors fit properly? Is the storage area open or enclosed?

Quality of material: Are the metal parts thick and sturdy or thin and flimsy? If it is portable, are the wheels made of crack-proof, weather-resistant material? Is the stainless steel 304 or 316 grade and heavy gauge? Is the hood double-walled stainless steel (single-walled will discolor)? If it's single-walled, is it enameled to preserve the metal?

Ease of movement: For portable units, try rolling the grill or smoker on the showroom floor. The wheels should be large enough to turn easily and to traverse uneven ground or cracks in a concrete, brick, or fieldstone surface.

Details and safety: Look for welds that have been polished smooth. Avoid grills or smokers with any sharp points or edges at eye, hand, or thigh level. Look for enough space between the handle and hood surface

so that your hand will fit through easily and safely. The handle itself should be made of a material that won't heat up during cooking.

Cooking grates should be heavy and sturdy: Stainless steel or porcelain-coated stainless steel or cast iron resist rust and clean more easily, but some cooks prefer the simplicity and weight of plain cast iron, which sears foods very well but must be more carefully maintained. (Oil the grates well before using the grill for the first time and oil them again before putting the grill away for the winter.)

A thermometer: Whether it's built in or portable, you'll want this to track the temperature inside the closed grill.

Workspace: In freestanding setups, having two side shelves provides some close-to-hand workspace.

Know the brand and your local retailer: How long have both been around? Particularly if you're buying a high-end grill or smoker, you want to know that there will be somebody to service it down the road, to respond to any problems, and to honor the warranty.

A portable gas grill with a covered side burner and a portable charcoal kettle grill make this outdoor kitchen ready for anything. The worktable, at far left, functions as counter space. On the right, the powder-coated aluminum dining table and chairs provide a place to enjoy the results.

What size cooking surface is right for you?

Here's my rule of thumb: If you cook on a 30-in. to 36-in. cooktop or range indoors and find it big enough for most meals, about the same size surface will probably work well for your outdoor grill, especially if you are making steaks or burgers, fish, or poultry. Not convinced? Consider that food on a grill sits edge to edge, without pots and pans or burner areas to take up any of the available cooking space.

However, if you routinely cut up and grill lots of vegetables, or whole corn on the cob, or large pieces of meat or poultry such as a butterflied turkey or a couple of spatch-cocked chickens at once, you may need a larger grill surface or be prepared to grill in batches. The same is true if you routinely cook for a crowd. Some grill cooks suggest that bigger is also better if you are in the habit of moving food around to take advantage of hotter and cooler grill areas. Keep in mind, however, that the amount of charcoal or gas you'll need to heat the grill has a direct relation to the size of the cooking surface.

Another way of thinking about grill size: Grill size is also expressed in square inches of cooking space, and this is how grill manufacturers tend to talk about it. A. Cort Sinnes, author of *The New Gas Grill Gourmet,* suggests that 350 sq. in. to 400 sq. in. is the minimum cooking area needed for serious cooks who like to make several dishes simultaneously. The HPBA (Hearth, Patio & Barbecue Association), an industry group, says that 400 sq. in. is the minimum and those who have larger families or entertain often may want 600 sq. in.

Charcoal grills

Charcoal grills have passionate advocates, and it's easy to see why. They deal with a live fire, skillfully controlling the heat, and their food tastes wonderfully sweet and smoky.

WHAT TO LOOK FOR WHEN PICKING A CHARCOAL GRILL

In addition to considering overall quality, sturdiness of construction, and brand and dealer reliability, here are some guidelines for shopping for a charcoal grill.

Check the way temperature is controlled: In grills with fixed charcoal grates, look for adjustable air vents at both top and bottom for maximum control. In addition, built-in

---

Keep the Fire in the Grill

Whenever you're dealing with high heat or live fire, be cautious. Set freestanding grills and smokers at least 15 in. away from buildings and be aware of materials in the area that can burn. Read the literature that comes with your grill and make sure you provide the necessary clearances. If you are in any doubt about the safety of your proposed installation, consult with your local fire department while you are still in the planning stages.

When ordering built-in equipment, such as a grill, side burner, or smoker, take care to order the appropriate model for your installation—insulated for installation into a combustible surround such as wood, or uninsulated for a noncombustible surround like masonry.

Store fuel intelligently—place extra propane cylinders in cool, shady locations, out of the main traffic flow, not in your home or a garage you use for cars.

Keep matches out of reach of children and always keep a fire extinguisher nearby.

Use sturdy, long-handled tools and inflammable oven mitts that offer real protection, such as those made of leather (available in hearth stores).

Clean the burners of a gas grill regularly with a long-handled brush to dislodge any spider webs that might have formed, which may block the flow of gas.

When installing permanent live-fire cooking equipment such as a masonry oven, follow the installation directions to the letter to ensure safety.

Don't leave fires unattended and use spark guards where appropriate.

One of the more interesting developments in outdoor cooking equipment is that manufacturers of high-end interior appliances have now extended their expertise and equipment lines to include outdoor kitchens.

In fact, many of these well-known interior appliance manufacturers produce whole integrated lines of equipment for the outdoor kitchen. If you are planning a complete outdoor kitchen, one advantage of buying such an integrated line is that everything is scaled, finished, and designed to go together. You may also be able to get a price break from the dealer on a package of appliances.

charcoal grills should have an adjustable grate to allow you to change the distance between heat source and food.

See if there is a way to add charcoal while cooking: In freestanding grills, this would be a hinged upper grate for access to the charcoal grate; in built-in or large grills, it's a side door or pull-out drawer that allows you to add fresh charcoal.

Make sure there is a comfortable, heatproof handle to raise and lower the lid: This should not hit or burn your forearm as you raise the lid.

Examine the ash pan: This is made to catch cinders before they hit the ground or deck. See how easy it is to remove, empty, and replace. Note that deeper ash catchers need emptying less often.

FREESTANDING CHARCOAL GRILLS

Freestanding charcoal grills are available in a wider range of sizes than you might imagine. Tiny portable grills suit those who cook for one or two or cook in small spaces like a

balcony. More ambitious cooks can find big stainless steel stand-alone grills as beefy and imposing as the most elaborate gas grill, and there are lots of choices in between.

Barrel grills: As the name suggests, this type of grill resembles (and in some cases is actually made from) a metal barrel. In the most basic form, the charcoal rests on a grate in the bottom of a barrel turned sideways, and a larger grate above holds the food. The top of the barrel is hinged to create a lid. They have the advantage of a large cooking area and relatively low cost. Like the dome grills discussed later, they can also be used as smokers and ovens, but the slightly more elaborate model that puts the charcoal in a separate side box makes for a much more effective smoker when cooking slow and low.

Dome grills: This classic form offers grill masters several different ways to cook: roasting and baking, direct heat grilling, and smoking. Materials range from the enameled steel of Weber's® kettle grill and Brinkmann's® smoker grill to kamado-shaped

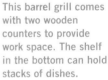

This barrel grill comes with two wooden counters to provide work space. The shelf in the bottom can hold stacks of dishes.

grills like the Big Green Egg® (BGE) and the Primo®. When the heat-reflecting domed lid is closed, foods cook via convection (heat circulates in the enclosed airspace) as well as by direct heat from the burning charcoal. In both metal kettle and egg-shaped grills, the heat is controlled not by the position of the grate, but by the draft control on the lid (which limits the amount of air that can exit the burning chamber) and the bottom vents, which control air intake.

All domed grills also work as smokers. In the Weber kettle grill you can smoke food by using indirect heat and adding presoaked wood chips to the charcoal, if you wish, to intensify the smoked flavor, whereas the Brinkmann is a classic water smoker, with heat and wood chips on the bottom tier, a water pan in the middle, and food on the top rack.

All domed grills can be used for baking or roasting. Bread can bake on a baking stone and a roast can cook on a rack set over a drip pan. With this arrangement, the grill

functions like an indoor electric or gas oven, because the bottom of the food is protected from direct heat and the lid acts as a convection device, radiating the heat back down and around the food.

There are also gas-ignition domed charcoal grills in which small gas burners act only as firestarters; they are lit briefly to ignite the charcoal, which then serves as the main cooking fuel.

The Big Green Egg is a domed, glazed ceramic cooker fueled by lump charcoal. Based on a traditional Asian grill form called a kamado, it's a thick-walled (1½ in.) and thus heavily insulated combination grill, smoker, and oven. It is similar to the Weber in that the heat is controlled by manipulating vents at the top and bottom of the grill; it's different in that the top vent is an adjustable little chimney. The grill's heavyweight material and design hold and reflect heat effectively, eliminating hot spots and big fluctuations in temperature. The Big Green Egg functions as effectively as a smoker as it does a grill, because the shape of the cooker and the tight-fitting lid closely control the flow of air and smoke. Food cooks with little loss of moisture in a heat-controlled environment that can range from as low as 180° to as high as 800°. The BGE uses a remarkably small amount of fuel to produce succulent results.

High flat-topped grills: Among the category of high, flat-topped, covered portable charcoal grills, the Portable Kitchen® cast aluminum cooker has developed a cult following. With a now-retro design (but revolutionary for those times) unchanged from the 1950s, this attractive, heavy, cast-aluminum covered grill combines visual appeal and nonrusting durability. Like a domed grill, it radiates heat back down onto the food; there's also a vent in the lid to control the air and regulate the temperature, but because the aluminum is thick and the cover is tight fitting, the food has a pronounced smoky flavor.

PERMANENT BUILT-IN CHARCOAL GRILLS

A permanent built-in charcoal grill is essentially a firebox with a lid, designed to slide into a permanent installation such as an outdoor island or counter. A built-in offers all the attributes of a charcoal grill on wheels, but in a modular form. One feature you may want to look for is a hatch or drawer for adding charcoal without having to move the food to do so, and an easily operated crank for adjusting the distance between the burning charcoal and the food grates. Attractiveness also counts for a great deal in a permanent setup, and such grills are available in black, stainless steel, and even copper-topped models. When choosing a built-in grill, the quality of the metal is a key factor, with 304 or 316 grade, heavy-gauge stainless steel the gold standard.

Built-in grills are usually designed to work as smokers as well as grills; if this versatility is important to you, make sure the unit you are considering allows you to cook indirectly over low heat by offering a tight-fitting lid.

Pellet Grills

Grills that use wood pellets are the new kid on the block, benefiting from consumer familiarity with indoor pellet stoves. Like pellet stoves, they use an automatic feed auger to release the right amount of pellets into the furnace to keep the heat at a certain level. Because pellets are available in a variety of woods, you can choose the wood that has the aroma you want for whatever you are cooking. Many say that food cooked on such a grill has a better smoke taste than food cooked on gas or charcoal. Because there is no open flame, there is no chance of flare-ups. Such grills are economical; a 10-lb. bag of pellets may easily fuel more than five separate meals. Standard electric current powers the auger (so you need an electric outlet close by), and the heat can be set at high (450°), medium (325°), or low (200° to 220°), making it easy to put food on the grill, set the temperature, and walk away. They are available in freestanding and built-in configurations and can be used to smoke and roast as well as grill.

CHARCOAL STORAGE

When creating a permanent outdoor kitchen that includes a charcoal grill, you'll want a weather-tight storage cabinet for charcoal. Make it big enough to hold a couple of bags, at least one chimney starter, and your grill tools—brush, spatula, fork, spray bottle, etc. Such storage could be behind doors, in pull-out bins, or in roll-out garbage cans.

If your grill isn't permanent, consider the nearest dry storage place for the charcoal and plan on storing most of your equipment in the same place or in the kitchen for quick, easy access.

CLEANUP AND ASHES

Charcoal fires generate waste in the form of ash. Create an ash storage area to hold a fireproof covered bucket and an ash shovel. Also make space for grate brushes and other cleaning tools. You can save your ashes and use them judiciously to fertilize your garden

ABOVE: Pellet grills use convenient wood pellets for fuel, available in a choice of woods for added flavor. An electric auger feeds the fuel into the hopper automatically.

LEFT: The Portable Kitchen cast aluminum cooker has remained unchanged from its revolutionary 1950s design. Now looking fashionably retro, it's still a great backyard grill.

The Great Debate—Charcoal versus Gas

Charcoal and gas or propane grills each have their advantages and drawbacks.

Charcoal:
- Less expensive than comparable gas model
- Real smoke flavor
- Enjoyment of making and tending a real fire
- Dependent on a supply of charcoal at hand
- Fires can be hard to start
- Coals can take 20 minutes or more to reach cooking temperature
- Harder to control the level of heat
- Coals must be replenished for longer-cooking items
- Ashes must be cleared regularly for good drafting

Gas:
- Heats up rapidly; can preheat in 10 minutes
- Easy to control the heat
- More convenient for year-round grilling
- Steady fuel supply when cooking
- Often components can go in dishwasher
- Side burners available for cooking nongrilled dishes
- Rotisserie option available with electric hookup
- Often comes with side shelves and storage cabinet
- More expensive than comparable charcoal grills
- Can only get smoke flavor by adding soaked wood chips
- Fuel tank needs to be checked and filled regularly (if uses propane)

Because each kind of fuel offers different advantages, it's not uncommon to find outdoor kitchens with both types of cookers.

in spring or fall or to scatter on snow or ice in winter to make walkways less slippery. Otherwise, once they're totally cool (24 to 48 hours), bag them up and toss them out.

Gas grills

Forty-five years ago, when natural-gas grills were first introduced, they began an outdoor revolution that got even more popular in the 1970s, when propane grills came into their own. Finally, you could grill outside with the ease, precision, and speed of indoor cooking. Although there are endless arguments about which fuel source makes the better-tasting food, gas-grill aficionados are resolute in their appreciation of gas's ease of use. Today, the majority of grills sold in the United States are gas grills.

Gas grills are available in freestanding and permanent installations in a wide range of price points with a choice of liquid propane or natural gas. (LP comes in those familiar portable cylinders, whereas natural gas is only an option in regions with natural-gas availability—it's accessed by pipeline in many locales.) If you plan to use natural gas, buy a grill made for natural gas. Similarly, if you plan to use propane, buy a propane grill. If you move from an area that has only propane to one that has natural gas, you can buy a conversion kit, although the actual hookup should be done by a dealer or a service company, as it can be dangerous if not done correctly. Similarly, when you buy a built-in grill, you have to specify what kind of gas you plan to use; the grill will come with the appropriate attachment or conversion kit for your area, and this will be installed by a service company when your equipment is hooked up.

HOW GAS GRILLS WORK

Whether fueled by a permanent connection to natural gas or from a liquid propane tank, gas grills share a three-level cooking structure. At the lowest level are the burners, which generate the heat. Most full-size grills come with two or three burners (more, if they are huge or a rotisserie), which can be operated independently so that you can cook with indirect as well as direct heat. The burners consist of variously shaped tubes with small portholes similar to those on your gas stove, through which the gas flows to be ignited.

Just above the burners is a grease-management system, either a deflecting shield or a series of troughs created to direct fat away from the flame and into a collection area. Look carefully at this grease-management system when choosing a grill. The best systems are efficiently designed and easy to empty and clean.

Above the burners and grease-management system is a heat dispersal layer, which is there to create smoky flavors. This layer is lined with metal "flavor bars" or ceramic briquettes. (Lava rocks are rarely used these days, as they are notorious for flare-ups.) Above this is a cooking grid of stainless steel, enameled steel, porcelain-coated cast iron, or uncoated cast iron, which holds the food. The bars and briquettes serve the same purpose: to create a hot surface that will radiate heat upward onto the food, disperse it evenly over the entire cooking surface, and capture any food juices or fats, burning them and sending their flavorful smoke back into the food. As long as the burners are powerful enough to heat the surface well, any of these materials will do the job.

IS IT ALL IN THE BTUS?

Many gas grills advertise their BTUs (British Thermal Units, which measure how much heat is generated) as an indication of how powerful they are. In one sense, this is correct, because a high-BTU burner will indeed cook food at higher temperatures and thus more rapidly than a less powerful model. However, there are a number of variables that can complicate the picture. For example, a high-BTU grill may have too much power, wasting gas at a great rate. Alternatively, a grill may have powerful burners but they may be placed so far from the grate (or be insulated from the grate by an awkward grease-management system) that it takes a long time to heat the grill. Finally, a smaller grill will require less power than a larger grill, so there is a func-

tional ratio between BTUs and size. Some grill manufacturers so dislike the whole BTU question that they have come to call it "better thermal utilization" to distinguish intelligent design from raw power. Experts say, in practice, that for all but the very largest grills or the coldest climates, a total of 35,000 BTUs to 45,000 BTUs is more than adequate for good grilling.

Still, when purchasing a gas grill you may want to compare BTUs between grills of similar size, thinking about the relationship between the power of the burners, the distance from the grate, and the size and weight of the grill. Ask the dealer how long

All about Infrared

Infrared is a heated ceramic or stainless steel surface surrounding the burner that radiates intensely high heat (close to 2,000°) to the food's surface. Think of infrared as a broiler, because that's essentially how it functions. Some gas grills are all infrared on every burner; they're capable of generating more intense heat (good for steaks, for example) quicker (in five minutes with some models), but (in less expensive versions) can be harder to dial down for slower-cooking foods (such as a whole chicken). TEC®, the leading infrared grill company, has introduced a new technology that eliminates the ceramic surround in favor of a glass layer between the heat and the food. The radiant waves pass through the glass to cook the food and no air ever reaches the food to dry it out. It's likely that the future will bring other new variations on infrared techniques from different manufacturers.

Alternatively, gas grills may have infrared as a feature in only one particular part of the grill, such as the rotisserie or as a high-heat separate burner, so you can sear on one part of the grill, then move the food to another area for less intense heat. In some versions, the infrared cooks like a restaurant salamander (or a broiler), from the top down. When the heat source is located above, there are no flare-ups.

Infared grills offer intense heat for flash grilling and and roasting, cooking food fast to create lots of flavor.

BELOW: It's not just about the grill: Side burners add versatility to outdoor cooking. Here, they're used to toast pita bread while kebobs cook on the grill on the left.

FACING PAGE: A wok burner is an option from some manufacturers, made to fit over a gas side burner. It consists of a broad ring that cradles the round bottom of a wok. Because the wok sits close to the flame, a cook can stir-fry properly over high heat.

it takes to preheat the grill—that can be an indication of how well designed the burners are for that particular grill. If it's longer than about 20 minutes, be concerned.

Gas grills have an inherent flexibility, because you can control the heat of each burner with a flick of the dial. You can set some parts of the grill at a lower heat than others for cooking different foods at the same time. This makes sense, because you may be grilling steak at high heat on one side of the grill while cooking thin slices eggplant and tomatoes on the other half. Independent burner control is also important if you want to be able to cook indirectly, in which case the food is placed over the burners that have been turned off.

WHAT TO LOOK FOR WHEN BUYING A GAS GRILL

As indicated in the general guidelines for any grill or smoker on p. 57, pay attention to the materials used in the body of the grill, the quality of overall construction, and the grate materials.

For gas grills in particular, do the following:

Note the number of burners: As each burner can be used independently, you'll have more flexibility with more burners—most grills will have at least two or three, and huge grills can have as many as six, with additional side burners to cook non-grilled items, as well as a rotisserie burner. Also note the BTUs of each burner to determine the total amount of grill power so you can compare grills with others of similar power.

Look at the controls: They should be easy to read and to use. Ignition systems can be initiated by electronic igniters, which do not require an electric outlet, or various clickers, which generate sparks. All of these work, but you may have a preference; electronic

ignition, which functions just like an indoor gas burner, is the newest version outdoors.

Check out the grease-management system: See how hard or easy it is to clean.

Can you lift the grill easily without burning yourself? Does it stay up without a problem?

Check out optional features: Before you pay extra money for them, give some thought to how important they are to you. Here are some add-ons you'll find offered:

- Infrared burner and/or infrared rotisserie
- "Dual fuel" option for adding charcoal or a place—usually a box or a tray—for adding soaked wood chips or to hold a foil package of pellets if you want to be able to use the grill as a smoker
- Side shelves
- Rotisserie: Fitted with a long rod, baskets, or forks at each end and connected to an electric motor, a rotisserie rotates food in front or on top of a hot (often infrared) burner, self-basting as it turns. It typically extends across the width of a grill and can easily spit-roast a turkey or a couple of chickens at one time.
- Side burners: Gas burners built into one or both sides of a grill, these are typically

one burner wide and one or two burners deep. They are useful for cooking marinades down into sauces and preparing side starches and vegetables that aren't grilled. See whether they come with a protective weatherproof lid or cover.

- Wok station: A side burner that has been modified to hold a round-bottom wok, a wok station allows you to stir-fry over high heat outdoors.
- Griddle: Many companies offer a griddle sized to fit over side burners or the grill cooking grid to create a griddle station for an outdoor breakfast or to quick-cook small bits of foods such as shrimp or mushrooms.

PORTABLE AND FREESTANDING GAS GRILLS

Far and away the choice of most consumers, freestanding gas grills may be offered with lots of bells and whistles at price points that vary widely. Interestingly, even with so many different gas grills available, more than three-quarters of all gas grills sold in America cost less than $300.

Small portable gas grills: Very small, lightweight, and truly portable grills are used for picnics, camping, tailgate parties, and

Warming Drawers

Built-in undercounter electric warming drawers offer a couple of advantages to outdoor cooks—they can be used to heat plates or coffee cups on chilly evenings and they keep cooked food warm. Warming drawers are also useful for proofing bread or pizza dough that will be going into your wood-fired oven. Because they have a moist and dry setting, these drawers can keep food crisp or prevent moist food from drying out (there's often a water reservoir that adds moisture to the air). Their temperature range is roughly 90° to 240°, and they come in sizes that match standard-size gas grills (27 in., 30 in., and 36 in., although this varies by brand).

Freestanding gas grills can also have warming drawers—a number of grill manufacturers offer them as an option for inclusion in a grill cart.

Stainless steel commercial-style racks, pans, and lids made to fit perfectly inside the warming drawer unit to hold your food at temperature are a useful accessory and are worth buying from your warming drawer manufacturer.

Two warming drawers are stacked below the gas grill on the left. They're useful features to have, keeping food and plates hot, and can even be used for rising pizza dough that'll be going into a wood-fired oven.

in places with limited space, such as apartment balconies (when such grills are allowed). Their small size makes it possible to build an outdoor kitchen almost anywhere, whether temporary or permanent.

There are lots of choices in this category—many are high quality and made of stainless steel, and some even come with

By surrounding a portable gas grill with counters and other equipment, you can have the convenience of a built-in kitchen

infrared burners to make grilling on the go as fast, hot, and convenient as it is at home.

Freestanding gas grills: Freestanding grills are much bigger than portables, and although they have wheels, they are not necessarily light or even very mobile—many of these grills are behemoths weighing as much as 400 pounds and take a great deal of effort to move. Nearly all freestanding gas grills have some storage space built into their base cabinets.

If you are transitioning from an outdoor kitchen with a freestanding grill that you love to a new permanent built-in setup, be aware that many high-end freestanding grill manufacturers also offer their grills in built-in versions. Know too that you may be able to customize the cabinet with options such as a warming drawer, small refrigerator, or sink.

Flat-top gas grills: One of the newest kinds of gas grills are flat-top solid grilling surface models (like a griddle), which are the outdoor equivalent of restaurant kitchen flat-top burners. The advantage of a solid-surface grill is that there are absolutely no flare-ups, it's easy to clean, and there's lots of flexibility in cooking. For instance, if you want a smoky flavor, you simply burn wood chips on the grill surface while the cover is closed, laying the food to be smoked nearby. Flat-top gas grills are available in both free-standing and built-in models.

PERMANENT (BUILT-IN) GAS GRILLS

For many people, building an outdoor kitchen begins with a permanent, built-in gas grill. Designed for counter or island installation, these grills come in a range of sizes from 27 in. up to about 48 in. You can also get side burners to install nearby from just about all of the manufacturers, and many grills come with an electric-powered rotisserie. Like any built-in grill, these are essentially boxes that are made to fit into or onto a grill cabinet or masonry surround. When you order a built-in gas grill, you'll have to choose your model in either

Putting Your Grill Together

Most high-end grills arrive already assembled for you or are delivered by someone who will put your grill together and place it on site as part of the package. With less expensive grills you may have to do the assembly, so unless your new grill is extremely easy to put together, consider paying the dealer to deliver as well as assemble the grill. For many people, this is money well spent. (However, check to see how well-assembled the grills are at the dealer—if they aren't, chances are they won't do much better putting together your grill.) Note that many home centers now offer grill assembly at no charge, just like upscale specialty retailers. Alternatively, some manufacturers have developed grills that they say take less than half an hour to assemble and don't require special tools.

insulated form (for use with a combustible surround like wood) or noncombustible and uninsulated (for use with a heatproof material). Built-in grills are set in place by your contractor and, if propane-fueled, are click-connected to a standard cylinder by the homeowner, because, even if built in, LP-fueled gas grills normally operate on the same propane tanks that freestanding grills use.

Propane Cylinders and Safety

Although liquid propane cylinders provide about 12 to 18 hours of continuous use, it is always a good idea to have an extra full cylinder on hand. Keep your extra filled cylinder out of the house— use a storage shed, detached garage (only if you don't keep your car in it), or shaded, low-traffic outdoor area.

Also, because propane is heavier than air, if there is a leak it will travel downward. For this reason, some communities have regulations governing whether or not you can put a gas grill on a balcony located above living spaces.

Built-in grills made for a natural-gas connection require a specialist to hook them up. Your gas company will insist that they do the work, or they will send you to a designated professional for the job (in some localities, this may be a plumber). In places where natural gas is available, you'll need to consult your local company to find out what you need to do to connect to it and to determine the cost (which will vary by locale). The line must be trenched and buried, with the route marked for safety's sake. In short, be certain to consult local regulations and your local gas company before proceeding to ensure that your planned installation is safe and according to code.

Electric grills
High-performance electric grills were created for a new market—those prohibited from having gas or charcoal grills, such as condominium owners or apartment dwellers with balconies who have to abide by "no open flame" rules.

What makes these new electric grills high performance is their ability to put out lots of heat and reach temperatures of about

LEFT: Some manufacturers of flat-top grills offer the option of direct and indirect cooking, with an outer circle of burners that can be turned off. Close the hood and you can roast, steam, warm, or smoke foods.

600° in 10 minutes or less. The level of heat is controlled by a thermostat (like an electric oven), so it's easy to set and maintain cooking temperatures. An electric grill (which requires either 110v or 220v) is a lot like a gas grill—it has a powerful heating element sited underneath metal grates, giving food seared-in grill marks. A high-performance electric grill using regular house current will cook just as well as an equivalent gas grill; the difference is one of size (the electric grill is smaller). The exception is the 220v-powered Electri-Chef®, which is the size of a big gas grill.

Beyond the Grill: Other Forms of Outdoor Cooking

There are lots of other ways to cook outdoors besides grilling: You can smoke foods in low, slow heat; flash-roast or make nearly instant pizza in the high heat of a masonry oven; or reduce a whole hog to fork-tender succulence in the top-down heat of a roasting box. Each of these cookers offers flavors you simply can't achieve with indoor residential equipment.

Smokers

Real barbecue isn't grilling—it's smoking. Traditional smokers were (and still can be) homemade affairs constructed from salvage metal or old metal drums, or made by digging a pit in the ground, building a fire, laying food near the coals, and covering the whole thing so the food can slow-cook in a smoky atmosphere. These are indirect cookers because whatever's cooking in them isn't exposed directly to the source of heat. (The exception to this rule is food smoked in an egg-shaped or kamodo-style smoker/grill—e.g., the Big Green Egg—which is actually exposed to very low direct heat,

albeit at a good distance from the coals.) The guiding principle, whatever the type of smoker, is this: Food that is smoked cooks at a low temperature (around 250° or less) for a long time in the presence of smoke.

That's why, when a covered grill is being used as a smoker, the hot coals are pushed to one side and the food is placed next to the fire, not directly over it. You can place a drip pan filled with water under the food to keep the drippings from burning on the hot metal and to add moisture to the air for more succulence.

Smokers of every design can and have been made at home using scrap materials. There are many websites that offer plans and help in building your own smoker; go to http://bbq.about.com/od/plansforsmokers for links to a number of sites.

Smokers fall into one of two types of designs: horizontal offset smokers and vertical smokers. Within the vertical category there

ABOVE: Powerful electric grills such as this one are especially useful for city dwellers cooking on balconies.

RIGHT: Portable propane hot plates are usually used for deep-frying, but can also be used, as this one is, for boiling lobster. Outdoor kitchens offer diverse opportunities for many kinds of cooking methods.

are vertical water smokers (which use a pan of water to keep things cool and moist) and box-style smokers (which are available in built-in models for outdoor kitchen under-counter installations).

OFFSET SMOKERS

Large in size, offset smokers are divided into three parts: the firebox (set lower than the smoking chamber, because smoke rises), a horizontal smoking chamber where the food is held, and an exhaust chimney. Some versions have an additional vertical smoking

A freestanding offset firebox smoker slow cooks food, giving it an exceptionally deep, smoky flavor, thanks to its internal baffle design.

Pick Your Fuel

You can add that smoky flavor to your food in a number of ways when you're smoking.

  Wood chips or chunks: Many smokers derive their wood flavor through the use of soaked wood chips, chunks of aromatic wood, or Bradley's® "wood biscuits." You can add wood directly to a charcoal smoker, but take care when adding it to either a gas or electric smoker, because you need to keep wood ash away from the gas burner so you don't clog the portholes, or away from the electric element so you don't damage it.

  Wood pellets: Pellet smokers offer a choice of wood flavors, from apple to hickory, and have internal augers, which feed the pellets automatically into the firing chamber, making them no-fuss smokers. You can turn a pellet smoker on, set the temperature, and walk away, checking it periodically.

  Logs: Big smokers that burn logs or sticks of wood for fuel tend to be those used on the competitive barbecue circuit, often towed on trailers, to cook massive amounts of food at one time. Some manufacturers offer smaller versions for the backyard enthusiast, with features like a water reservoir for added succulence and a propane log igniter for ease of use.

chamber (often fitted with niceties like sausage hooks). The primary advantage of an offset smoker is that it has internal baffles designed to control and route the smoke from the firebox into the smoking chamber, where it circulates around the food, then exits through the chimney. An offset smoker can also offer versatility—in some models you can build a fire in the smoking chamber and use it directly as a grill.

VERTICAL WATER SMOKERS

Water smokers can be powered by charcoal, gas, or electricity. They are easy to use and can smoke everything from cheese to chicken or ham. As much as 10 lb. of charcoal can be stored in the fuel area to keep the smoker cooking for a long time, although more charcoal can be added later if necessary. The rate of combustion is controlled by the air intake, aimed at maintaining a long, slow, smoky fire. A benefit of a water smoker is that the added moisture in the chamber helps to keep the

chamber cool, control meat shrinkage, and add succulence.

A water smoker typically looks like a little silo or missile—it is, essentially, a cylinder mounted on short legs, its interior divided into three parts. The bottom area holds the heat source, in the central area is a pan of water, and the top holds the food and a small chimney. Some water smokers are constructed as a single-piece cylinder, which makes them less versatile. Look for models with three separate stacking sections, which allows you to remove the water pan, move the cooking grid down, and grill on the grate over the coals.

BOX SMOKERS

Box smokers look like refrigerators. Commercial versions powered by gas or elec-

tricity use woodsmoke from a smoldering source in the bottom that circulates throughout the smoker before exiting. Available in stainless steel or black enamel, they offer a precise, worry-free smoking at-

When you build a fire in a masonry oven, you construct a log cabin of twigs and small branches in the center of the oven floor. Gradually, you add slightly larger pieces of dry wood, keeping the fire centered in the oven. As the oven heats up, the domed ceiling may turn white, or an integral probe thermometer or portable laser thermometer can be used to see if you've achieved temperature (typically 600° to 750°). At this point, any burning logs are pushed to the rear of the oven to provide smoke and continued heat, the hearth is swept clean, and cooking commences either directly on the oven floor (for pizza) or in a pan placed on the oven floor.

mosphere, because you turn the smoker on, set the temperature, and walk away. These are available in undercounter sizes with a small smokestack that projects through the counter. You can also get larger models that are freestanding, made to use alone or to build into an outdoor kitchen like a refrigerator (albeit with a smokestack). Although there are also charcoal models available, electric and gas-fueled smokers maintain a steady temperature and require less attention than charcoal smokers because you don't have to check the fuel supply.

Outdoor masonry ovens

In contrast to our American tradition of barbecuing, people in France and Italy have long cooked outdoors in freestanding wood-fired ovens. They are extremely versatile structures because you can bake, high-heat roast, and even grill (with a rack insert over the coals) in them, depending on the temperature inside and whether you are cooking with the door open or closed.

A masonry oven is an igloo-shaped structure made of cast refectory (high heat–resistant) materials, much like fire-

brick. It is designed to withstand intense heat (up to 700° to 800°) and to hold the heat for long periods, which is why most are installed with a thick layer of insulation. A chimney typically projects from above the front opening or (alternatively) just above the front cavity at roof level.

Although these ovens are traditionally heated with a wood fire, some models are now available with gas burners. You can

When Winter Comes

If you live in an area where winter means living indoors, you'll want to protect your outdoor equipment for the season. You can buy covers from the manufacturer, made to perfectly fit your grill or smoker. These are strong enough to leave outdoors in even the harshest climates.

Unplug all electrical appliances big and small, and, if you can't move them indoors, cover them well with plastic to keep them dry.

Protect side burners with the covers they come with, or with purchased metal lids or weatherproof covers, and close up any open cooking areas, such as fireplaces, masonry ovens, or fire pits, to keep them clean and dry, using the covers they come with or other appropriate materials.

If your outdoor kitchen is in a gazebo or pavilion or under a shed roof, you may want to consider making winter shutters out of plywood or canvas to keep the worst of the weather out.

Right-Out-of-the-Box Pizza Oven

Pappa'z Pizza Oven is a one-piece, painted (terra-cotta color) cast cement oven made in South Africa. It is the only wood-fired pizza oven I know of that is ready to use right out of the box (no assembly or building needed, no permanent installation required).

It comes with and sits on a metal framework with short legs, which should be placed on a table covered with cement board or other inflammable covering. It weighs about 450 lb. and can be moved by two or three people. Because it is one piece and uninsulated, it doesn't hold heat well and so is limited to the rapid cooking of pizza rather than items requiring longer cooking. Also, it can be hard to know when it has reached a sufficiently high temperature to commence cooking, unless you have a laser thermometer to check the temperature.

Pappa'z Pizza Oven is ready to use without any building or installation. Its great benefit is that it heats up much more rapidly than more expensive, built-in masonry ovens. This blazing fire went from kindling to cooking in just under an hour.

buy wood-fired ovens already assembled and delivered to your site or in kits that must be assembled and insulated on site. Any mason can easily put a wood-fired oven kit together for you; many are designed to be installed by a handy homeowner and come with printed and video directions. In addition, there are custom builders of outdoor masonry ovens as well as books and instructions you can buy to build one yourself (see Resources on p. 224).

To find such a builder, contact local masons, look on the Internet, and consult books on masonry ovens. Often oven builders will travel across the country to custom build or know of other oven builders in your region. Every oven kit comes with safe-installation instructions and most also comply with California's stringent earthquake and fire codes. As with any chimney, local rules for clearances near buildings need to be taken into account.

To use an outdoor oven, build a hot fire out of small, then increasingly heavy pieces of wood over a two- or three-hour period. (If you are just making pizza in an out-of-the-box uninsulated oven, the oven should be hot enough in less than an hour.) When the oven reaches about 700° or the interior dome turns white, rake the coals to the rear, sweep the hearth, then cook directly on the hearth. If you keep a log burning in the back, you can cook a number of pizzas. If you close the oven door to keep the heat in, you can roast meats or poultry, and if you allow the oven to cool somewhat, you can bake bread in it. In my wood-fired oven we like to do all three things in sequence, ending with a terra-cotta pot full of beans and water set in the oven overnight to cook in the falling heat for the next day's dinner. The flavor of food cooked in a wood oven is incomparable.

FACING PAGE: Nearly all masonry oven kits have to be assembled with mortar and enclosed. This one was built into a little house, complete with its own peaked roof. A light near the peak illuminates the mouth of the oven. The area below the oven is used to store wood.

FREESTANDING MASONRY GRILLS AND GRILL/OVEN COMBINATIONS

Several importers offer beautiful masonry grills and grill/oven combinations that are practically complete outdoor kitchens (they don't have sinks or refrigerators). They look romantic and Old World, yet arrive as cast modular components ready to be assembled by homeowner or mason.

Caja china

Based on a Cuban tradition, one of the newest outdoor cooking novelties to hit the U.S. market is called a caja china. A roasting box on wheels, it is lined with stainless steel and fitted with a top tray to hold burning charcoal. The interior of the roasting box has two metal grids, which sandwich the meat between them; it is traditionally used to cook a whole butterflied pig, though you can use it to cook poultry, roasts, and racks of ribs as well. The meat is cooked indirectly from the top down and must be turned midway through cooking. Cajas come in three sizes, ranging in capacity from an 18-lb. turkey to a 100-lb. pig. You should select a caja according to the amount of food you plan to cook in it at any one time,

Caja china is a stainless steel-lined roasting box based on a Cuban design. Meat that has been split (or butterflied) is placed in the box, sandwiched between two wire grill plates. Charcoal burns on the steel tray on the tip of the box, creating a oven with top heat (much like a broiler). Because the box is closed and the meat split, whole pigs or lambs or turkeys cook rapidly; the meat is turned once during cooking.

because the amount of charcoal you'll need is determined by the size of the box, not what's being cooked inside it. My advice: Unless you plan on roasting a whole pig often, buy the smallest size and cook roasts and poultry instead. Cajas need to be assembled (a fairly easy process).

Picking the Fire That Is Right for You

How you like to cook and eat is key to the equipment you choose. If you love smoked flavors, you'll probably be happiest with a smoker/grill, a smoker, or a charcoal grill. If you're cooking outside every day, a gas-fueled infrared grill will do the job at top speed. If you love playing with fire, you'll be unhappy with anything but a charcoal grill, a masonry oven, or a log-fueled smoker or campfire. If big parties that feature cooking whole hogs are your thing, a caja china is a must. And if you're dreaming big, maybe you'd like to have a setup that includes both a charcoal and gas grill as well as a wood-fired oven.

Having it all can be less expensive than you think, particularly if it's not a permanent built-in kitchen. A good charcoal grill, gas grill, and portable pizza oven can be had for $3,000 to $4,000, depending primarily on the price of the gas grill you choose. If cooking with gas is not on your wish list, you can opt for an all-in-one masonry grill/oven combo, getting it all in one neat package.

On the other hand, it's useful to remember that you can make extraordinary food on a charcoal grill or small gas grill costing $100 or less. Outdoor cooking does not have to be about expensive equipment or elaborate setups. It should be about the great pleasure of cooking outdoors and the company of friends or family.

Because this family uses their outdoor kitchen almost every night, they chose a big gas grill for fast and easy cooking.

An Intimate Santa Fe Courtyard Kitchen

Cheryl and Bill Jamison are expert barbecue chefs, cookbook authors, and three-time winners of the prestigious James Beard Award for excellence in cookbooks. They've written more than a half dozen cookbooks focused on outdoor cooking, as well as another half dozen notable cookbooks devoted to other aspects of American home cooking. All their outdoor recipes are created and tested in their Santa Fe, N.M., outdoor kitchen.

ABOVE: Shrimp, soft-shell crabs, and salmon sizzle on the gas grill while artichokes and tomatoes wait on the counter. The integral bullnose on the tiles create a seamless front edge to the counter.

LEFT: Used as a fireplace, the masonry oven heats the dining area on chilly nights. Weathered teak furniture sits near a fragrant lilac, decorated with twinkle lights. The coyote fence is visible behind the stucco wall.

Their home, a converted adobe dairy barn surrounded by fruit trees, features an enclosed courtyard kitchen with a unique masonry fireplace that's a cross between a Tuscan grill oven and a traditional rounded New Mexican kiva fireplace used for warmth and for cooking. "We wanted to have the look and feel of a traditional New Mexican fireplace, but with the added benefit of another place to cook," says Cheryl.

As outdoor cooking experts, they've had as many as fourteen different grills and smokers cycle in and out of the courtyard as they've tested recipes. These days, they've given most of those cookers away to friends and now keep their outdoor kitchen relatively simple: just a grill, a smoker, and the fireplace for cooking. They have chosen to do without a sink, refrigerator, or other appliances, because their outdoor kitchen is located immediately outside their interior kitchen door.

"We really wanted to keep it simple," says Jamison. "It's our garden and a living area, not a kitchen, and we wanted to keep that feeling."

The kitchen illustrates lots of thoughtful features: a counter of handcrafted California tile made with an integral bullnose front, which makes the front edge much less prone to chipping, a backsplash of patterned Mexican tile, a sturdy patio floor made from Colorado red flagstone, and built-in raised planting beds for a variety of herbs and flowers. Other personal touches include a wooden plum-drying rack from the south of France mounted on the wall above the kitchen counter and a twig coyote fence made of cedar poles and wire (a traditional barrier that still functions to keep coyotes out), which rises above the stucco wall that surrounds the courtyard.

The courtyard is formed by two wings of the house, creating an intimate setting for the kitchen and dining areas. The other two walls are made of stucco backed with coyote fencing. Mixed plantings of daylilies, coreopsis, helianthus, and lavender offer scent and blooms.

ABOVE: Centered around a Mexican carved stone fountain bought from a local dealer, the living room area of the garden is all about relaxing and slowing down. It's a good place to husk corn too. The coyote fence is visible behind the stucco wall, and staked low-voltage landscape lighting illuminates the plantings that edge the patio.

RIGHT: Water spurts from the mouth of the fish, lands in the small basin, and then rains down into the larger pool, making a symphony of cooling water music.

At night, a single hooded low-voltage landscape light makes lavender stalks glow and highlights their texture. The pool of light it sheds shows how effective even a small amount of electric light is outdoors. Santa Fe has strict light-pollution regulations and this light illustrates the power of a downlight fixture.

FACING PAGE: Looking into the garden from over the back gate, the sinuous curves of the oven and wall show why New Mexican style is so revered and often imitated. The garden seating pulls you in from the back entrance to the garden courtyard, and lavender bushes on both sides of the path provide their alluring astringent scent and vibrant color. The rustic ladder is a traditional New Mexican piece.

ABOVE: To the left of the kitchen door and the outdoor kitchen counter, a long stucco retaining wall offers seating. The garden behind it is planted with colorful coleus, which thrive in partial shade.

ABOVE RIGHT: Cooking rotisserie chicken over a pan of rosemary potatoes is great culinary multitasking. The natural gas grill's rotisserie works off a nearby electric outlet set into the front of the kitchen counter surround.

RIGHT: Salvaged antique doors capped by a wooden portal frame the way into the breezeway that connects the main house to a guesthouse. The topiary is boxwood underplanted with variegated vinca. Also visible are the outlines of the original mortared adobe brick, dating to the 1920s.

Urban Oasis

There's a thriving group of outdoor cooks in Chicago who are so committed to the pleasures of live fire and high-heat dishes that they even cook through Chicago's harsh winters. Perhaps the best known of these is famed chef and restaurateur Rick Bayless, who owns Frontera Grill and Topolobampo. He is also the star of the PBS series *Mexico: One Plate at a Time* and the award-winning author of six cookbooks. He and his wife Deann and daughter Lanie use this urban outdoor kitchen for family meals and weekend entertaining.

Their home, a 1916 former tavern in a neighborhood just beyond Chicago's downtown, sits on the equivalent of three city lots. About a thousand square feet of the area is a production garden planted with heirloom tomatoes, baby greens, and chili peppers that are used in the restaurants, and another thousand

ABOVE: Hot Mexican chili peppers grow well in this handmade pot, where the soil quality and degree of moisture can be closely controlled.

FACING PAGE: A delicate Chinese paper parasol adds an exotic touch to this umbrella table. Although not made to withstand harsh weather, such parasols offer dappled shade and great beauty.

RIGHT: Arched cavities under the counter hold baskets of kindling and tools like the rotisserie, and a wooden door beneath the wood-fired oven keeps logs dry. Arranged along three legs, the outdoor kitchen offers ample counter space. Tall streetlamp-style down lights mounted on poles illuminate cooking and food preparation.

FACING PAGE: Located just beyond the stairs that connect to the indoor kitchen, this outdoor kitchen is conveniently sited for bringing tableware and foodstuffs in and out. The stainless steel double sink makes it easy to wash vegetables from the garden before putting them on the grill.

square feet are used to grow flowers for the table. The family's outdoor kitchen is built in the shadow of two old maple trees, in a spot that had always been a problem to landscape. By siting the outdoor kitchen there, they turned a negative into a positive.

The kitchen is set on flagstones and grass and located near the home's back stairs and indoor kitchen. It's arranged in a series of angled runs that form a shape something like a backwards C. It contains an under-mounted stainless steel sink with hot and cold water, an undercounter refrigerator, a gas grill with a side burner, and a wood-fired oven, along with generous counter and serving space. Rick just recently replaced a conventional built-in wood oven with the less expensive cast-cement Pappa'z Pizza Oven.

Its advantage is that it heats up rapidly, allowing for impromptu wood-fired cooking. Says Bayless, "I love that I can light it up and be cooking in under an hour."

A masonry base constructed from local limestone supports Vermont soapstone counters, which Rick carefully oils very lightly (too much would stain guests' clothes) with mineral oil before each party for a fresh finish. There's an umbrella table near the kitchen, with additional seating around the garden, and a second dining area under the grape-covered pergola on the deck behind the garage. When the family is entertaining outside, strings of lights create a party mood, along with bright Mexican textiles and twinkling candles and torches.

FAR LEFT: Off the back of the garage, an expansive deck under a grape-and-wisteria-covered pergola is used for parties and relaxation. Often, this is where the adults sit while the children gather near the outdoor kitchen and the table there. Torches light up the night and contribute to the festive mood.

LEFT: Beyond the outdoor kitchen, the rest of the property is used for cultivating vegetables, herbs, and flowers for Rick's restaurants. The stone path invites guests to wander.

BELOW: Vertical planting makes this urban farm productive; heirloom tomatoes flourish growing up a wire trellis. The marigolds are used both to deter insects and for the tables of the restaurant.

Deckside Cooking

Chef and restaurateur Michael McCarty is one of the founders of California cuisine, which celebrates the bounty of fresh and seasonal produce. Owner of the eponymous Michael's restaurants in Santa Monica and New York, he is also a well-known art collector (even his restaurants are filled with paintings). Inside and outside, his home reflects his modernist sensibility and his passion for good design.

ABOVE: Arranged in a cooking line, the outdoor kitchen features a gas grill and masonry oven. The countertops are made of the same granite used in the indoor kitchen, which helps to link both kitchens and creates a more seamless cooking experience.

LEFT: Looking down the hillside planted with grapes, the outdoor kitchen is in the foreground. Striped umbrellas define the seating areas facing the ocean view, and the tall evergreens provide shade and a windbreak.

McCarty, his wife Kim, and their two children live in a contemporary house in Malibu overlooking the ocean. Surrounded by steep vineyard plantings of pinot noir grapes, the house has a huge deck that's used for frequent entertaining. Like a restaurant kitchen, the outdoor kitchen is arranged in a line for greatest efficiency, and features a gas grill and wood-burning oven, along with counter space for food preparation and plating. Because this kitchen is open to the rest of the deck, a number of cooks can work at different stations simultaneously, as in a restaurant. Wooden cabinets hold tools and equipment close to hand under the counters. Beyond the kitchen's back half-wall, grapevines climb the hill in orderly rows, contributing beauty and atmosphere.

The rest of the deck is devoted to dining and seating for lots of guests—there are five umbrellas that shelter tables, and the chairs and chaise longues are sited to take advantage of the ocean view. Under the deck, which is a story above the ground, there are garages and living spaces.

RIGHT: This sliding window in the indoor kitchen makes it simple to pass prepped food out to be cooked, and to receive cooked food when eating indoors. This kind of pass-through is invaluable when the outdoor kitchen is also used to prepare food eaten indoors, and when food to be cooked in the outdoor kitchen is prepped indoors.

BELOW: Rosemary in full bloom scents the air as well as foods cooked on the grill.

FACING PAGE: At dusk, when the fog rolls in, the landscape looks like a Japanese print. Diners stay warm, however, thanks to the glass half-walls on the deck, which shield them from wind coming off the ocean.

LEFT: This wood-burning masonry oven is encased in whitewashed stucco and has a steel door. It is a restaurant-grade model, made in France.

BELOW: The strong lines of the front chimney breast create dramatic shadows on the face of the masonry oven.

Beyond the Grill:
Outdoor Appliances, Cabinets, and Counters

Although your outdoor kitchen could easily contain only a grill, there's a world of off-the-shelf equipment available for outdoor use: sinks, refrigerators, counters, and much more.

These items are particularly useful if you cook outdoors every day, or if your outdoor kitchen is a distance from your indoor kitchen. The choices you make about equipment will determine the scale and size of your outdoor kitchen and (if you are planning a built-in kitchen) your cabinet requirements. Equipment choices will also have a major impact on your budget, so make these decisions early. As when planning an indoor kitchen, you may have to decide what's most important

FACING PAGE: With plenty of storage, a sink, side burners, and a gas grill, this all-in-one-line outdoor kitchen has lots of cooking areas and counter space. Flexible headlight lamps can bend and turn to illuminate the cooking areas.

for you—appliances or cabinetry—and adjust your budget priorities accordingly.

There is, however, a simpler option for an outdoor kitchen. Unlike indoors, you can actually buy one-piece "complete" outdoor kitchens that may include the additional equipment you think most important, thus bypassing bigger and more expensive cabinet and equipment quandaries. Read on to see what you might want to consider.

Just like an indoor kitchen, each of the equipment choices that follow are dropped into cabinets made to accommodate them (grills, side burners, and sinks), or slid into cavities or cabinets (refrigerators, beverage centers). Every cabinet line made for outdoor kitchens offers cabinets for these specific purposes and you need only to bring your equipment choices or specifications to the dealer to get the right cabinet for the job.

If you are custom building a surround for your built-in appliances, keep in mind that every equipment dealer and manufacturer website has installation information that details the exact measurements of each piece of equipment and offers painstaking instructions on safe installation. Whether you order cabinets from a dealer, a manufacturer, or

your contractor, all of them will refer to these measurements and instructions for installation.

You can mix and match the pieces of equipment you want, or because they come in standard off-the-shelf sizes you can leave space for them as you plan your cabinets or surround and add them later over time as your budget permits.

The Cold Zone: Keeping It Cool

Outdoor kitchens are used mostly when the weather is warm, so keeping food cold is essential, both for food safety and for freshness. There is a surprising variety of specialty appliances made for cold storage. Note that all of these electric appliances run on regular household current and will require GFCI three-prong grounded outlets nearby, so you need to plan your electrical needs accordingly.

Refrigerators

A number of companies manufacture under-counter refrigerators that are UL®-listed for outdoor use. Typically, they are designed without a freezer section and are relatively small (5 cu. ft. to 6 cu. ft. or so). Because

of their size, they are not meant to hold the full array of food stowed in an indoor fridge—rather, only the items you'll be using in the outdoor kitchen that day, such as meat that's marinating for the grill, cheeses or dips for hors d'oeuvres, or soda, wine, or beer. (If you feel you need more cold storage space, you could always have two, side by side.) The great advantage of an outdoor refrigerator is that it offers close-at-hand cold storage for immediate use.

There are variations in style and construction among brands of outdoor refrigerators (glass versus stainless steel doors, refrigerators that are all drawers), so research brands and compare prices, as there are big differences.

Some of these models are available with casters for a freestanding option, but most are made as undercounter built-ins. For a permanent outdoor kitchen, you need only leave the required space (usually 24 in.) between other cabinets or between uprights to accommodate a refrigerator, along with a strategically placed electrical outlet to plug it into. If the fridge vents to the front, you need not make any other allowances, but if it has a back vent you may need to drill

This beverage refrigerator in an outdoor bar counter is a real convenience when entertaining.

some holes in the back of your cabinet or surround to give the waste heat a place to exit. Check the installation instructions or talk with the dealer to be sure of the best way to install a refrigerator for a long life.

All-beverage refrigerators

Also available are all-beverage refrigerators, usually designed to hold cans in the middle section and with two shelves for wine—one on the bottom (to keep it chilled) and the other on the top shelf (to keep it at serving temperature, because, even in a refrigerator, warmer air rises).

Off-Season Storage for Outdoor Appliances

In cold areas where an outdoor kitchen is unused in winter, unplug all major appliances until spring and store portable appliances in an enclosed garage or shed, if possible. In climates where temperatures soar in summer and that's when you stay inside in air-conditioned comfort and don't use your outdoor kitchen, consider cleaning, emptying, and unplugging your cooling appliances in weather that's routinely over 100°.

Wine coolers

Wine coolers or wine cellars are small, glass-door refrigerators fitted with wire racks for holding wine bottles horizontally. Typically, red wine is stored on the upper shelves, with white wine below that, and champagne on the bottom and chilliest shelf. A 24-in.-wide model generally holds about 48 bottles.

Half-keg beer dispensers

These refrigerated dispensers hold half or quarter kegs, which decant into a draft tower that comes with a CO_2 tank and regulator. Many of these are available with wheels, so they can be used as portable dispensers as well.

All of these units are between 15 in. and 24 in. wide and are made to be used in outdoor temperatures ranging between 45° and 100°. (In areas that regularly reach temperatures higher than 100° for weeks at a time, refrigerators will be working hard and risk overheating.)

Refrigerators and wine coolers that are made for undercabinet installations have reversible doors so they can be installed with right- or left-hand swings.

Ice makers

If you entertain often, love drinking very cold beverages, or live in a very hot place, you'll want an outdoor ice maker. They offer what can feel like a limitless supply of "crys-tal clear" ice (up to 35 lb. a day can be made and stored, on average, for built-in models). Like indoor units, they defrost automatically. A typical model is 15 in. wide and requires both a drain and a water hookup.

In contrast, a portable unit does not require installation—you just plug it in and add water to the reservoir. No drain is required and some units make up to 29 lb. of ice in a day, although they are too small to store a whole day's production.

The Hot Zone: Getting the Heat Out

Grilling, smoking, even cooking on a side burner—all of these generate smoke, heat, and grease. When you're cooking completely out in the open, this is not usually a problem, but when you're under some kind of shelter or roof, these by-products can build up unpleasantly.

Exhaust systems

If your grill or smoker is installed under a roof, such as on a porch or in a semi-enclosed building like a pavilion, you may want to consider installing an exhaust hood or fan to pull smoke, heat, and odors out of the space and into the great outdoors. Grill manufacturers have anticipated this need, and several supply hoods that are made for outdoor cooking. You should make sure that any exhaust system you consider is approved for outdoor use, because even under a roof an outdoor kitchen is considerably damper than an indoor version. All exhaust fans are electrically powered, so you'll need a junction box near the fan site to connect it. This is a new category of exhaust system use and it's sure to expand in years to come. As of now, the choice of outdoor hood styles is limited to classic boxy models, but they may become more varied over time.

CUPOLAS OR VENTING SKYLIGHTS

A cupola attached to a semi-enclosed building or a venting skylight added to a porch roof will act as a heat chimney and draw heat, grease, and smoke upward and out of the building. Because hot air naturally rises, this option does not require an electrical connection (unless you are using an operating skylight with a remote control).

CEILING FAN

If you *are* planning electrical connections, however, you may also want to add a ceiling fan that is UL-listed for outdoor use. The great advantage of such a fan is that it moves air rapidly, giving you more control over the venting process. Place the fan in a central position, near a skylight or cupola, if you have one, for maximum efficiency. If

you don't have an exit in the roof, don't install an overhead fan—it will only blow the smoke around and not help it exhaust.

The Wet Zone: Outdoor Sinks

Outdoor sinks are available in many different materials, sizes, and styles: as freestanding multipurpose "beverage centers" or "refreshment centers," on wheels for portability, or for built-in installations. If you want a sink, your first decision will be whether to build one into a permanent outdoor kitchen or to go the portable route. Your next choice will be whether to have only cold water available (which means you can use a garden hose hookup) or hot water as well (which will require running a water line from the house), so that you can wash dishes outside. Finally, you'll need to decide

cost. Freestanding sinks, such as those included in beverage or refreshment centers, come as one-piece units that do not demand cutouts, as is also the case with portable sinks.

Beverage or refreshment centers

Beverage or refreshment centers are multi-purpose units that contain a small sink, condiment bins, bottle openers that catch caps, decks and shelves for bottles and glassware, some additional storage, and trash containers. Some also include a built-in filtration system to turn garden-hose water hookups into better-tasting water. These centers are really made for outdoor bar areas.

Portable sinks

Completely portable sinks are available in standard single- or double-compartment configurations made to connect to a garden hose, or in more specialized sizes and materials. They are meant for hand washing and cleaning utensils, and some models hold their own waste water in containers that

ABOVE: The sink in this kitchen connects to the home's water system through the common wall at the rear, an inexpensive way to have water outdoors. It is well protected by the roofed alcove that surrounds it, and can be drained in winter, if desired.

RIGHT: Refreshment centers like this one are well set up for entertaining. In addition to the sink, condiment bins, and ice bucket sink, there's a bottle-cap opener on the front face of the unit (with a cap-catcher bin below), as well as a towel holder.

how you will drain the waste water; if you want it to be routed to your septic system or dry well, this will be a more expensive option (requiring the digging of trenches and laying pipe) than draining it into a gravel- or stone-filled area, diverting the water to your garden as gray water, or storing waste water in a tank that you empty. If you want to use your gray water, be sure to use a biodegradable soap that will not harm your plants. For permanent installations in climates that freeze in winter, you'll need to design in an easy way to drain the pipes every autumn, by installing a spigot at the place where the water line connects to your house line.

Be aware that a built-in sink has implications for your counter expenses, because some sinks will require cutouts in the counter, which can increase the overall counter

you empty at the end of the day, eliminating the need for any plumbing lines. Other portable models offer cooling, too, in the form of an insulated ice bin that drains through a plug.

Built-in outdoor sinks

Many sinks made for interior kitchens will work well outside, because sinks, by definition, are made to withstand wet, though not all can tolerate freezing. In cold climates with freezing temperatures, drain your sink of all water before the temperature drops and cover it with a tied-down or weighted tarp or plastic sheeting to keep any rain or snow out.

SINK MATERIALS

Stainless steel is always a safe choice because it does not corrode, and is nearly the universal choice for portable and one-piece outdoor sinks.

For built-in installations, porcelain sinks, which are actually enameled steel, are also a good bet. Those made of real porcelain ceramic (also called fireclay) or enameled cast iron are not, except in mild climates, because they can crack in freezing weather.

Copper sinks are an increasingly popular outdoor choice, as outdoor weathering accelerates the development of a lovely natural patina.

Stone sinks such as those made of slate or soapstone are also good choices for out of doors and are available in sizes big enough to wash a half-bushel of leeks fresh from the garden.

Man-made materials such as Corian® are also useful and sturdy outdoors. Corian can be made into a seamless sink and counter combination, and is also strong enough to use structurally to support a grill, for example.

This Danish outdoor kitchen is made of stainless steel and wood. It's meant to be used as a complete kitchen—the green plastic tub is filled with water and used as a sink and the hot plate is used for outdoor cooking. Handy hooks hold tools and equipment.

Sink styles for built-in installations

These sinks are only made for built-in installations; they are not available as freestanding options, because they are made to be part of a countertop. They are essentially the same choices available when choosing a sink for your interior kitchen.

- *Drop-in sinks* have a flat lip that surrounds the sink and overhangs the counter. This style will have the lowest cutout price (the cost of cutting a hole out of the countertop material to hold the sink), because the lip hides any imperfections in the cut.
- *Undermounted sinks* are attached from below the counter with clips and have as their upper edge the cutout of the counter material. They look beautiful and don't have that hard-to-keep-clean edge where the sink meets the counter surface like drop-ins do. Cutouts for undermounted sinks are always more expensive, because they have to be perfect.

"scrap stone" runs of counter on each side of them (see p. 112), rather than a more expensive long run of counter that needs a cutout.

- *Integral outdoor sinks* can be made of Corian, concrete, or stainless steel. They are fabricated in one piece. They have no edges that demand finicky cleaning attention and they need no cutouts, because they are part of the counter.

SINK SIZES AND BOWL STYLES

Many manufacturers seem to think that outdoor sinks should be diminutive. Certainly, the sinks in refreshment centers are tiny, as are the many copper and stainless steel "bar sinks" that many people install in their outdoor kitchens. My own opinion is that bigger is better. My ideal outdoor sink would be a stone apron-front sink that is 20 in. front to back, 30 in. side to side, and

ABOVE: Enameled steel porcelain sinks are fine for the outdoors, and this is a particularly attractive installation. Note how the cap on the backsplash creates a narrow shelf for serving.

RIGHT: Corian is a good material for the outdoors because it's impervious to weather. Here, a Corian integral sink and counter make a seamless outdoor wet zone.

- *Apron-front or farmhouse sinks* are free-standing in relation to the counter—the sink is completely visible in front and the counter runs up to it on each side (and can slightly overlap), but it's not hung from the counter and the counter is not cut out to accommodate it. Because apron-front sinks are made to meet the front plane of the counter, they have no counter area in front of them. Sometimes they have an area of counter behind the sink—this is called a back deck and it's where a faucet is usually placed. Alternatively, an apron-front sink may have a high back, which is a kind of integral backsplash and is made to accommodate a wall-mounted faucet.

The advantages of an apron-front sink are many: You get less back strain, because you can belly up to the front of the sink. They also come in large sizes with greater depth. Finally, for outdoor kitchens on a budget, you can use short

9 in. to 10 in. deep, although a sink that is as large but has a shallower configuration is wonderful for washing vegetables and scrubbing grates. Such shallow sinks offer great functionality in an outdoor kitchen, where food preparation (rather then dish-washing) is the primary sink use.

FAUCETS

Stainless steel makes sense for its weather resistance, but consider a material like uncoated brass (though it is hard to find and you may end up searching salvage yards or stripping coated brass to get the look), which can age and develop a patina with outdoor use. Faucets can cost a lot or a little, and one thing that makes a price difference is the quality of the materials. If you want the best, look for solid brass fixtures with a thick coat of chrome, brushed nickel, or enamel, fitted with a ceramic disk. On the other hand, you may not need or want a top-quality faucet for an outdoor kitchen that is not used daily all year round. This is where you can save money by buying an inexpensive faucet that can be easily replaced as needed.

Talking Trash

Trash is a topic that needs attention when planning an outdoor kitchen, lest you end up with a fabulous kitchen decorated with a black trash bag on the floor.

Some manufacturers offer a dedicated pull-out trash cabinet as part of their cabinet line, and they are also available as freestanding units. Site-built alternatives include sizing an opening to hold a trash can or, alternatively, you could mount an automatic-opening trash can to the cabinet and to the door. Attractive stainless steel

Restaurant Equipment for the Outdoor Kitchen

Restaurant supply houses, especially those that sell used items, are an economical source for outdoor kitchen equipment. Here are some pieces to be on the look out for:

- Prefabricated one-piece sinks on legs can easily fit into an outdoor configuration. Made of weather-impervious stainless steel, they can be found both new and used.
- Big stainless steel restaurant worktables, fitted with a lower shelf and/or wheels, make terrific islands, workstations, or portable counters.
- Small commercial worktables can be set up alongside grills for plating and serving space.
- Heavy-duty restaurant-quality spring-loaded tongs with long handles make working with food on the fire safer and cooler.
- Elbow-length oven mitts make it harder for the grill master and fire maiden to burn themselves.
- Stainless steel utility bowls in a range of sizes from tiny to enormous make outdoor kitchen life easier by giving the cook a place to toss lots of vegetables in olive oil before laying them on the grill.

Putting It All Together: Cabinets and Counters

You can construct an outdoor kitchen using individual cabinets ganged together (just like an indoor kitchen), or you can build a surround for your appliances and make as many or as few openings in the base for storage as you wish, with or without doors on them.

In an outdoor kitchen, the primary function of cabinets is essentially architectural—they make the structure of the "room" by linking the appliances together into a whole. That's why an outdoor kitchen can consist only of a freestanding grill, or a built-in grill cabinet that holds nothing other than a propane tank (this is the only really necessary cabinet for function in the outdoor kitchen). Of course, it's wonderful to have as much storage as possible, for everything from hot mitts to tongs to serving platters, but it's not as essential as it is indoors, because so many elements of outdoor food are already traveling from indoors out.

The other function of outdoor cabinets is to provide a surface to put a counter on for working space. Again, this is an amenity, not a necessity—often, pull-up side shelves or a worktable on wheels may offer enough counter space.

You can buy cabinets for outdoor use in both stock and semicustom sizes, and in a couple of different materials. You can also build (or have built) a custom surround for your built-in outdoor kitchen appliances out of a number of materials: stacked masonry elements such as brick or block, which can be covered with stucco or other materials; cement board covered with cultured stone; stone tile; or other weatherproof materials suitable for your climate, such as ceramic tile in areas that do not freeze. You can also buy cabinets to connect side by side to cre-

The custom masonry surround of this barbecue is beautiful, but the only storage it has is for kindling, which is placed under the grill.

trash cans are widely available in lots of sizes and styles. I suggest you mount one on a custom-made plywood round (sized to fit just inside the underside of the can). Screw the plywood to the can, add casters to the plywood, and you've got a mobile trash can that can follow you around the outdoor kitchen as you need it. Use plastic trash can liners for ease of emptying. In a built-in kitchen, leave a base cabinet cavity big enough for the can (make sure not to let it be too tall) and you'll have a garbage garage to keep the can in when it's not in use.

ate a custom island (or other configuration), or purchase completely ready-made islands, which can contain storage, appliances, and a wealth of other options.

Custom masonry

Particularly in warm-weather climates such as California and the Southwest, you'll see lots of outdoor kitchens built of masonry elements. These are beautiful and are perhaps the quintessential outdoor kitchens, because they hark back to traditional ways of building and ornamenting cooking spaces. However, these structures are fairly monolithic and only have cabinets and doors where necessary, such as under the grill to access the gas cylinder. That's because the building elements themselves take up lots of space, leaving surprisingly small cavities to use for storage. It can also be difficult to find doors or drawers that are both suitable for outdoors and sized to fit such relatively small openings.

DOORS AND DRAWERS FOR MASONRY CABINETS

If you have a masonry island made for your grill and/or other appliances, you will have the option of buying stainless steel doors from your grill manufacturer in sizes scaled for setting under the grill (for example, to hide an LP gas cylinder). If you want other cabinet doors or drawers for a custom setup, you can buy them from the grill manufacturer or have them fabricated for you. Materials to consider are stainless steel, a weather-resistant wood such as teak or redwood, or painted exterior-grade wood siding or plywood. Custom metalwork for doors or counters is often available from roofing or sheet metal dealers (look in your local yellow pages); cabinetmakers can fabricate drawers or cabinet fronts out of

your choice of wood—be sure to tell them that it's an exterior application, so the wood is appropriate and suitably finished for weather protection.

Building blocks: Ready-made kitchen cabinets

You can purchase ready-made outdoor kitchen cabinets for installation in a complete built-in outdoor kitchen, or for a permanent island application. (Some dealers offer these with a countertop option. If not, usually a template is made for a counter after the cabinets have been installed, to ensure that it is cut properly for the site.)

Outdoor cabinets are constructed so they won't warp, rot, or split in an outdoor environment, as well as being colorfast and UV-protected. Of necessity, these cabinets have to be extremely solid. This is a whole new category of cabinet manufacturing and will probably explode in the coming years, with even more choices than presently available.

Outdoor ready-made cabinets are completely self-supporting and can be set next to one another along one side of the house,

---

Walk on the Wild Side: Keeping Nature at Bay

When designing and building your outdoor kitchen, as well as maintaining it, think about nature, wild in tooth and claw. Insects and field mice can lodge in grill cabinets, and spiders often clog gas burners (and can present a real safety hazard—use a small flexible grill brush regularly to dislodge spider webs). If you plan to keep any food outdoors, construct tight cabinets and keep everything in hard-to-open screw-top and airtight containers. Always clean up scrupulously and don't invite wildlife into the area by leaving crumbs behind for them to forage. Overhead fans help to discourage insects (though only while they are moving), and daily use of your kitchen will make most creatures hide or flee. As for those sonic devices meant to discourage field mice, bats, chipmunks, squirrels, and the like, I've not had much success with them.

Polished granite counters reflect light and the shadows of trees in this poolside outdoor kitchen. The dining bar bump-up shields any cooking mess from the view of those outside the kitchen.

arranged in an ell or U-shape on a porch or patio, placed along four walls of a custom pavilion, or set in any other configuration you choose. They can also be freestanding, positioned to make a custom island or freeform arrangement that suits your space and needs. There are special cabinets made to hold grills, sinks, and refreshment centers, as well as a full array of storage cabinets with pull-out shelves, drawers, or both. Although you could theoretically take the cabinets with you should you move, once you've installed them with permanent counters, plumbing, and electricity, they are not very portable. Think of them as the building blocks for a permanent, built-in outdoor kitchen.

At this time, ready-made or semicustom outdoor cabinets are available in three categories of materials (in order of increasing price): a plastic polymer similar to what is used to make plastic cutting boards (and which comes in colors) for the shell and the cabinet fronts, polymer cabinets with a wood (teak or cypress) front option, or a plastic core covered in stainless steel on the exterior with a white plastic melamine-like interior.

Ready-made means that the cabinets are available in stock sizes and colors and are constructed to fit into a space by the use of filler strips to mask any gaps. Semicustom cabinets also come in stock sizes, but you may be able to customize them by adding more drawers or making the sink cabinet accommodate an apron-front model. Semi-custom cabinets will take several weeks to arrive, whereas ready-made cabinets may ship immediately.

Ready-made appliance islands

Many manufacturers have large and small complete "islands" or one-piece portable kitchens you can buy off the shelf. Their great advantages are that they are often portable, they offer a fixed-price choice (great for budget control), and there is a huge range of sizes and styles available. These come entirely finished and need no further counters or other elements, aside from a flat surface to put them on and perhaps an electrical connection, a garden hose, or a source of light for evening cooking.

At the simplest end of the scale are grills on wheels with storage cabinets, and some even offer a sink that hooks up to a garden hose. At the other end are grill islands that feature high-quality stainless steel counters, drawers, and doors in configurations that provide counter space on either side of the grill, with storage below.

Many dealers and manufacturers will allow you to customize their islands by replacing a cabinet with a small refrigerator or adding a garden hose sink, whereas others may offer complete package deals that are convenient and may cost less than their individual components.

Countertop materials

Once you've chosen your cabinets, it's time to decide on a countertop, assuming you're creating a built-in kitchen. There are lots of materials suitable for outdoor use: In dry climates, consider woods such as teak or cedar. In temperate climates, you can use ceramic tiles (which are not an option in more northern climes, as they can freeze and crack). In every setting you can use poured concrete, granite, slate, soapstone, or stainless steel. Let's look at each of these materials in turn:

- Weather-resistant woods such as teak, cypress, mahogany, and cedar are slightly waxy in feel when new; they age to a rough gray texture unless protected by a regularly renewed oil finish. They are more suitable for cabinet fronts than for counters, as they may cup, split, or warp when made into counters.
- Poured concrete can be stained, aged, custom colored, polished, or waxed to make an extremely beautiful counter in an outdoor kitchen. Waxed concrete can show stains if exposed to water, so only

use wax as a finish in enclosed, weather-protected outdoor kitchens. Concrete contractors, kitchen counter fabricators, or other specialty builders may make custom concrete counters, which is a relatively new purpose for this material. (See Resources on p. 224 for books on the subject.)

- Granite, available in polished and honed versions in a wide array of colors, is a very hard and durable counter material. Polished granite will hold up best out of doors.
- Slate is an inherently strong stone for counters and slabs of slate are a particularly nice choice for overhangs like a bar counter, because the grain of the stone is long and ledge-like. It comes in a range of colors from gray to green to purple. It should be treated with a stone sealer.
- Soapstone can be used for outdoor kitchen counters, but will require regular (at least monthly) applications of mineral oil in season. After oiling, it's a matte charcoal gray-black. A soft stone, it needs a lot of support in the form of metal or wooden brackets when used as a dining bar overhang.
- Stainless steel is a wonderful counter material for indoors or out because it is so

ABOVE: Durable materials are essential for outdoor kitchens. Here, the counters are made of slate tiles, as is the floor. Brick carcasses fitted with steel doors make the supports for this kitchen.

LEFT: Because the gas grill and counter are sheltered by the back wall of the house and deep porch roof, the butcher block counter is protected from weather.

easily sanitized, it's food safe, and it's not subject to corrosion, though it is prone to scratching. It needs to be dry polished with a towel to stay shiny and should be fabricated with a lip at the edge of the counter to keep spills from dripping onto the floor.

- Copper, which comes in sheets, is less expensive then you might imagine. It will patinate and age to a dull brown with green blotches, or can be painted with a verdigris compound to hurry the aging process. Alternatively, it can be polished to a high sheen, which will need to be repolished regularly—at least weekly. You can also have copper polished and sealed to keep its sheen. Whether copper is sealed or finished or not, it is not a food-safe surface (even copper cookware is tinned on the inside). Use a cutting board between food and the counter.

Shelf brackets spray painted black support a soapstone dining bar.

Sensible Scrimping with "Scrap" Stone

Check out local quarries, stone fabricators, and even monument makers—often they have short runs of stone left over from other jobs that they will sell to you at a substantial discount. You might also want to consider using stone that is not square cut, but rather has raw edges, which offer a sculptural quality.

- Even less expensive is zinc sheeting, which can be formed into counters the same as copper. Like uncoated copper, zinc is not a food-safe surface. Zinc makes a stable surface that needs little attention, and will last for at least twenty or thirty years.

Check out building supply yards and garden centers—they offer a range of pavers, bluestone patio tiles, and preformed concrete units that can be used as less expensive counters for outdoor kitchens by adventurous homeowners.

COUNTER INTELLIGENCE: HOW IS IT PRICED?

Stone counters are usually priced by the linear counter-foot, which means that the price covers the cost of 1 ft. of a 25-in.- or 26-in.-deep counter. (The alternative way of pricing a counter is by the square foot, which means that the price of a counter-foot is twice the price of a square foot, because counters are typically 2 ft. deep.) The price becomes greater for stone with the choice of edge treatment (simpler is less expensive) and the number and complexity of cutouts required for appliances such as sinks.

Tile counters are priced by the piece (or

tile), with the exception of very small tiles available set on net backing—these are sold by the square foot. Edging elements, such as the curved front edge tiles known as bullnoses or other kinds of edge trim pieces, significantly raise the price of the counter, because they are always much more expensive than flat tiles with four raw edges. The cost of a tile counter is the cost of the tile plus the cost of installation, which is typically computed by the square foot.

Metal counters are priced by the cost of the sheet metal and labor, and can increase with the addition of a front lip (worth paying for, because it will keep spills on the counter, not dripping down the cabinet fronts or onto the floor), an integral sink, and/or a cove backsplash (which makes the backsplash meet the counter in a smooth, seamless curve). Cutouts for sinks or other appliances will also raise the price for metal counters, even if you are installing a drop-in (rather than undermounted) sink. Metal counters are fabricated at the shop and delivered to you in one piece for a straight run of counter.

Concrete counters are custom fabricated on site and you will be quoted an inclusive whole-job price that will include an integral sink (if that's what you've specified). Adding color, adding fossils or other inserts to the cast, constructing integral backsplashes, and so on will increase the total cost.

Wooden countertops will also be custom-made and their cost will reflect the cost of wood (these are expensive woods), which is sold by the linear foot, and the labor to fabricate and finish them.

As you plan your kitchen counter, if budget is a factor, try to make the design as economical as possible by limiting cutouts and edge treatments. Using short runs of material between appliances will always be

Countertops of stone add a shot of dramatic color and pattern to this kitchen, where the ceramic floor, walls, and stucco undercounter area are all monochromic variations on the same warm color.

less expensive than cutting into long runs. It will also allow you to mix materials, if desired. You could have a stainless sink and counter welded together as one complete unit (or you can buy such a unit—they're found in restaurant supply houses, both used and new), for instance, with short runs of "scrap" stone between the grill and the pizza oven to create a very useful outdoor kitchen with a much-lower-than-you-would-think price tag.

Get a Kitchen That Works for You

However you plan your outdoor kitchen, whatever you decide to include in it, know that there are great choices available in every price range. Your kitchen can be made of a number of completely mobile or freestanding units, it can be a single free-standing piece, or it can be permanent and built in. In each of these categories, you can choose the particular appliances, cabinets, and counters that suit your climate, your lifestyle, and your budget. These days, if you want a complete outdoor kitchen, manufacturers have created myriad options that allow you to have it all on your own terms, scaled for your pocket and desires.

Behind the Screen

This Maryland couple did an extraordinary thing: They built an outdoor kitchen that can be seen or not at the touch of an electronic button. Hidden behind a retractable weatherproof white metal hurricane screen, the kitchen is part of a pool-house complex that includes both living room seating and a dining area that can be housed under a sheltering roof, further protecting the kitchen area

ABOVE: The main house, with its bluestone-paved brick-walled terrace, has a screen porch and wide steps leading down to the pool and formal boxwood-edged parterres. The generous width of the steps provides gracious passage for a number of guests at one time, whereas many seating options offer guests a variety of places to perch. The pool house (not visible here) is located to the left.

LEFT: Echoing the architecture of the main house, the pool house's generous roof is supported with large columns. The depth of the roof provides further shelter for the indoor-grade cabinetry and appliances and shade for the sitting area, more than could be supplied by an umbrella, a real amenity in warm climates. The kitchen is visible at the rear.

ABOVE: Stacks of colored glass plates sit behind transparent glass doors, at the ready for a party and easy to find, thanks to the see-through cabinetry.

RIGHT: Inside the kitchen, the painted wood Shaker-style kitchen cabinets offer pullout shelves to provide convenient storage for table linens and the sound system controls. An interior-grade dishwasher adds further entertaining ease.

BELOW: When the hurricane screen is down, we can only see the sitting porch. You'd never know there is a kitchen behind the metal wall.

FACING PAGE: Even though it's outside, this kitchen is anything but rustic. Because of the weather protection provided by the hurricane screen, it was possible to use interior-grade stock cabinetry. The undermounted sink is stainless steel, with brushed nickel fixtures. The counters are polished Absolute Black granite. There are heaters concealed in the toe kick that are climate-controlled to preserve the cabinetry; they go on automatically when the temperature dips.

from the elements. When the owners want to access the kitchen's cabinets, refrigerator, sink, or dishwasher, they press a button and the screen glides silently upward. When they're done, the screen comes down.

The pool house, which also contains a bathroom and outdoor showers, visually complements the main house's elegant Georgian style, and looks back over the pool toward the house through a series of formal gardens. Adjacent to the house, above the pool, a wide bluestone terrace is used for more formal dining and for large parties. Because the pool house sits on one side of the pool below the terrace and is integrated with mixed plantings and paths, the whole pool garden area, terrace, and screen porch function together as extended entertaining space for the couple's frequent gatherings.

The grill is kept near the house for family parties, but big events are usually catered and, in that case, the outdoor kitchen functions as a bar area for cocktails and hors d'oeuvres and is also used for cleanup. When just the family is there, the pool-house kitchen is often used for lunches.

Patio dining is enhanced by the scent of roses, and the screen porch to the right offers a haven from insects. Mixed plantings add variety and dimension, as do the colorful containers and urns along the terrace.

ABOVE: Details make all the difference: Notice how the shutters and window box increase the allure of the pool house. Black shutters echo those on the main house, whereas plantation shutters on the inside of the window further filter summer's fierce sun. Hydrangeas offer mop heads of color.

RIGHT: A portable gas grill lives just outside the home's kitchen door, but can travel wherever it's needed. As it's usually used for family meals, it's most convenient to use it next to the interior kitchen.

Inside the porch, comfortable indoor/outdoor rattan seating enhances the pleasures of conversation, and the brick floor echoes the house's facade. The screen porch is used only in season; during the winter the pillows are stored in bags and the furniture is protected under covers.

The Resort Life at Home

ABOVE: In one corner of the patio, the kitchen island has its own palapa (grass umbrella), as well as bar seating. Nearby, a table and chairs benefit from the shade cast by the house.

FACING PAGE: Guests can enjoy their drinks at this poolside table at night. The rope lights inside the palapa don't add a great deal of illumination, but provide a party atmosphere.

When this family moved to southern California from Philadelphia, they didn't just change their address—they changed their whole lifestyle. Because San Diego has one of the most pleasant climates in the country, they now can revel in a year-round life out of doors. The backyard, which is centered around an inground swimming pool, is really their home. Except for sleeping, it's where family life happens, with a choice of places to relax and sunbathe, to enjoy a beverage and a bite to eat, to be in the company of others, or to find a moment of quiet meditation. This family cooks outside almost every night, often joined by friends.

The outdoor kitchen and dining areas have a relaxed, tropical feel, emphasized by the use of palapas, or thatched umbrellas, which keep guests cool. The kitchen island is sheltered under one

ABOVE: Adjacent to the island, the built-in gas grill can cook lots of food at one time. The outdoor light on the left swivels to illuminate the grill surface at night.

ABOVE RIGHT: A storage cabinet next to the refrigerator holds barware and a portable fan. Even though the house is close by, it's a real convenience to be able to keep some things outdoors.

RIGHT: The fire pit is close to the hot tub and pool. Because it was built higher than usual, it's very comfortable for sitting.

and includes a bar/counter, space for food preparation, and a refrigerator, as well as a storage cabinet. A built-in gas grill is nearby.

In another area, a gas-fueled fire pit was constructed 18 in. higher than usual to allow for comfortable sitting around its perimeter. Its center is piled with lava rocks, which glow like embers, but without the smoke. The hot tub and swimming pool offer further pleasures. Propane heaters extend comfort after sundown, as do the rope lights that twist and twinkle under the kitchen palapa. Colorful plantings edge the yard and contribute to the resort mood, making this family feel like they never need leave home to relax.

Under the palapa, dappled shade offers relief from the sun and keeps food and drinks cool. A bottle opener is mounted onto the palapa's pole. The slightly raised eating bar creates a boundary between the dining and food-preparation spaces.

ABOVE: Indoor-quality tableware, a tropical flower centerpiece, and fresh local food make outdoor dining special.

FAR LEFT: Looking outside from the indoor dining area, the pool is just steps away. The outdoor dining area is shaded under its own palapa, next to the bougainvillea that climbs the fence

LEFT: This small bar area gives the family another spot for entertaining. The freestanding bar and bar stools are made of powder-coated aluminum and fabric.

Al Fresco Dining with a View

ABOVE: Outdoors, saucepans are useful for cooking down marinades or for making rice or other grain dishes.

FACING PAGE: Built above a flagstone patio, the portal spans the width of the house and protects the interior from heat and sun. Locally made iron railings edge the stairs and balcony, and wooden columns topped with Santa Fe–style carved corbels support the roof. The parapet funnels rain off the roof and directs it to the cistern hidden below. Lavender, daylilies, spirea, and butterfly bushes thrive at the edge of the patio.

New Mexicans call porches *portals*, and they are typically built to be both deep and dark, to provide shelter from the intense sun. Bob Schwan, an artist, and his wife Nancy, a decorator, moved to Santa Fe from the Midwest. Like many who choose to settle in the Southwest, they cherish the traditional architecture unique to the area. As part of the renovation of their new home, they built a traditional portal. It was expressly designed to serve as their outdoor kitchen, dining room, and living room.

Complete with a breathtaking view of the Sangre de Christo Mountains, the portal faces northeast. In the early evening, the distant mountains reflect the sunset's colors, turning shades of mauve in the waning light. Built nearly a story above the garden

level, stairs connect a small garden dining patio with the larger living spaces on the porch.

Because the portal is deep, the light-loving homeowners have installed skylights in the roof to provide additional natural light during the day. Another innovation is the cistern fitted under the portal to collect rainwater for the garden. It's part of a massive 5,000-gallon gray-water system that recycles water for maximum use, a necessity in this desert environment.

ABOVE: Newly made in antique style, the concrete fountain on the lower patio provides a focal point and cooling sounds. The custom latticework behind it supports trumpet vines and roses, and is there to provide what Nancy calls "eye relief," a calming backdrop for the plants. To the right of the fountain, the café table is used for morning coffee, because this area is shaded when the portal is in full sun.

RIGHT: Just off the indoor living room at the other end of the portal, the outdoor kitchen and dining area take full advantage of far mountain views. One of Bob Schwan's paintings is hung above the gas grill. The ell-shaped kitchen has a refrigerator, grill, side burners, sink, and three-drawer storage unit. The slate tile counters offer durable work surfaces that contrast well with the stainless steel appliances and painted stucco of the surround.

FACING PAGE: Outdoor living rooms can be as comfortable as their indoor cousins, and this one has the added bonus of a kiva fireplace. Above the mantel, a Turkoman child's bib (used to ward off evil spirits) provides color and pattern. Hanging gourd lights from Mexico illuminate the far end of the space, and an iron Mexican lantern and tabletop candelabra provide further atmospheric light. The tile table is also Mexican, the shawl on the couch is from Guatemala, and the patchwork pillow is from India.

ABOVE: Set diagonally into the corner of the kitchen's ell shape, a surface-mounted stainless steel sink occupies "dead corner" counterspace that might otherwise be wasted. Slate tile has been set in a diagonal pattern for visual interest.

LEFT: Three drawers hold aprons, grill tools, and hot mitts, respectively. The stainless steel freestanding storage unit was purchased separately, then built into the custom surround.

FACING PAGE: Set against the iron railings, a pine bench is used for overflow seating when the couple entertains. A potted mandevilla vine underplanted with heliotrope makes this corner both fragrant and colorful.

Dining and Entertaining
in the Great Outdoors

What could be more pleasurable than entertaining outside? Whether on a condominium balcony or in a big backyard, nothing is better than enjoying good food and good company in the open air. Outdoor entertaining can range from a potluck barbecue to a formal wedding celebration, so it's useful to anticipate the whole range of possible activities when you plan your outdoor spaces. This chapter covers the gamut, from selecting and creating sites for conversation, dining, and entertaining to choosing furnishings and amenities such as fire pits, outdoor heaters, and insect-repelling systems. (For information on outdoor lighting and sound systems, see pages pp. 183–193.)

ABOVE: Courtyard kitchens and dining rooms have many benefits: They're close to the house, which minimizes trekking, and they're protected from wind as well as public view.

FACING PAGE: Stone walls and verdant plantings make this dining area private and quiet. Container plantings supply even more bloom, filling in the edges of the terrace and further muffling any ambient sound from the street.

A Place for a Little Help from Your Friends

Cooking outdoors is always a social event. Because friends like to hang out near the grill, make it comfortable by providing a place to perch, whether on chairs or a bench or at a sitting bar near the cook. In addition to socializing near the grill area, if space permits, you'll probably want an actual dining area conducive to leisurely eating and lingering.

At its simplest, a sitting bar is a prefabricated, contractor-built, or owner-built structure that incorporates a freestanding or permanent grill or smoker with counter areas on one or both sides and a nearby or parallel counter or bar, made for high stools or seats. It can be sheltered by an umbrella, awning, or permanent roof, and is often 4 ft. or 5 ft. in total length. The sitting bar serves two functions: It gives the cook elbow room and a designated stage and it provides an appreciative audience a place

to sit. Take care to site the sitting bar away from prevailing breezes, so you don't smoke your guests!

A sitting bar can also be a staging area for platters of food and stacks of plates, or a space for making or serving drinks as well as enjoying them. Be sure to add electrical outlets to the bar if making blender drinks is a vital part of your outdoor entertaining experience.

If you're a beer drinker, you may want to include a built-in beverage fridge, a portable cooler, or a designated place for a keg in your bar. If your outdoor kitchen is some distance from your indoor kitchen, you will also need a place to keep cans of soda or bottles of water chilled; you may also want an ice-cube maker.

Sitting pretty

Bar stools come in two sizes: counter height (25 in. to 26 in.), made for a standard 36-in.-high counter, and those that range from 29 in. to 31 in., for counters in the 40-in. height range. In contrast, regular chairs with seats 18 in. high are made for sitting at a table that is 29 in. to 30 in. high. Here's the rule: Allow at least 10 in. between the top of the stool and the counter for a comfortable perch.

Outdoor stools are available in all the usual outdoor furniture materials, including aluminum, PVC, wood composites, wrought iron, cedar, redwood, and teak. You can find stools with backs or backless, folding versions and those that do not collapse for storage, and in styles designed to be used with or without pads or cushions.

Dining in Comfort

If at all possible, locate your sit-down dining area far enough from the cooking area to put you and your guests out of range of the

Although a sitting bar is most often located along the outside edge of an outdoor kitchen, this Midwestern kitchen keeps diners under its sheltering roof.

smoke and mess. If your available space is limited, such as on a balcony or deck, there may be only one place to set a table and chairs. Backyards with a bit more space may offer more options, so keep in mind the following when choosing and planning a site:

Distance to your outdoor kitchen: Ideally, the dining area should be close enough to the cook site that transporting hot food from the grill is not a trek, yet far enough (and in the right direction) that prevailing winds will not send smoke to the table area.

Distance to your indoor kitchen: Even if all of the food is cooked outdoors, you will still be transporting table linens, silverware, dishes, and glassware (or their disposable equivalents) from house to outdoor table. You'll also be clearing the table and transporting all of these items back to the house (or the trash area), along with any leftover food, condiments, and platters to be washed. If you are lucky enough to have a level path and no steps between the house and outdoor dining area, you can use a serving cart, moving lots of dishes and glassware in one easy trip.

Topography: If you're blessed with a naturally flat area, you're in luck—setting up a

dining area will be easy. Otherwise, you'll need to make a level area by using earth-moving equipment and installing patio materials, or by building a wooden deck or platform.

Electrical Needs

Do you want to light your outdoor dining room with candles, torches, or kerosene lanterns? If so, you might want to build in some wall niches for candles or lanterns or think about places where iron hooks can be placed to hold hanging lanterns. Alternatively, you could build posts or other elements designed to hold hooks for strings of electric lights. If you think you want electric power, make sure to plan for a pedestal outlet, at a minimum (this is the least expensive electrical outlet for outdoors), which can support a string of lights and another electrical fixture such as a central electric lantern hung from a hook.

If you are planning a built structure with a roof and electrical connections, seriously consider adding outdoor-rated overhead fans—they can be an enormous asset in really hot weather. At the other end of the

LEFT: Built under a vine-covered pergola, this outdoor kitchen has a raised dining bar around the corner from the grill counter. Sturdy stools offer seating with a view of the cook.

BELOW: Woodland dining rooms offer a more rustic experience. Although this one is some distance from the house and the outdoor kitchen, its pleasures to its owners outweigh any disadvantages.

temperature scale, if you are thinking of a heater to extend the season, decide whether it will be a self-contained streetlamp-style LP gas heater or a smaller electric unit. If you choose an electric heater, be sure to plan for a 220v or 110v power outlet as appropriate.

Making the Best of a Not-Perfect Situation

Perhaps the best dining site you have is not attractive—maybe it's a dusty, flat patch of dirt or located in the side yard next to the utility pole or garbage cans. Think creatively —you could hide those unsightly garbage cans by surrounding them with a gated fence or lattice screen, then distract the eye by directing it elsewhere by making a focal point with a dramatic plant, sculpture, or fountain. Don't be afraid to use architectural elements such as columns or to add painted color. Plants can also add tremendous charm—try training flowering vines up strings or on a trellis, and use bloom-filled pots or boxes arranged around the borders of the space.

Public sites can be made less so

If your intended site is visible from the street or your neighbor's bedroom window, don't despair, you can still create privacy. To drown out traffic sounds or neighboring

conversations, plan for a trickling fountain, which will create white noise and help filter out other sounds. If your neighbor often entertains at top volume, site your dining area as far as possible from the boundary you share and plant a noise buffer of dense shrubs. For visual privacy, a structure with lattice or reed panels will let in breezes, yet shield you from casual view.

Differentiating the Dining Area from the Cooking Area

Define the dining area by thinking of it as an imaginary room. Even though an outdoor dining and entertaining space doesn't necessarily have actual walls or ceiling, it helps to conceive of it as if it were a separate place. Start by determining the size of the dining area, making sure to add at least 2 ft. to 3 ft. to all sides of a seating arrangement to guarantee ease of access and a feeling of generosity. Next, think about how to visually separate it from the cooking site.

Right: Custom lattice provides privacy from the neighbors at the end of this dining area. Its shaped rafters offer support for vines; as they grow and fill in, the courtyard will become even more private. Keeping the round moon windows clipped free of vines will prevent the space from feeling claustrophobic.

Marking the walls

If your dining area is on a deck, with the area already defined by the back of the house on one side and a railing on the other, you can set off the dining area with planter boxes or with a partial lattice wall and window. Another option might be to actually roof and screen in a portion of the deck, making an insect-free sheltered dining area that is separate from the cooking site. For visual privacy rather than insect protection,

LEFT: Bluestone slabs inset into a brick patio help to define the dining area and differentiate it from the rest of the terrace.

BELOW: Rosy pavers inset into gray flooring make this dining area stand out. Distant mountains form a glorious backdrop.

Signal it's a dining area with a change of flooring

If you're building a brick terrace, for example, you can have the dining area floor set in a herringbone pattern and the rest of the terrace in another pattern. You could do something similar with flagstone, changing from large squares on the perimeter to a smaller, more random pattern to form a rug in the dining room. A relatively easy way to define a dining area on a painted deck or porch is to mask off and paint the dining area in a different color. You could further elaborate this by painting and/or stenciling an outdoor "rug" to define the dining area.

Consider using more ephemeral materials than you would for the cooking area, as long as you are prepared to renew them periodically. Finely shredded bark can be spread on bare earth to form a cushioning floor, as can a layer of hay or straw. Even a grass mat or coir rug can serve to mask and civilize beaten earth and will last a season. New outdoor rugs made of weatherproof materials are available in a range of colors, sizes, and patterns. (For a more in-depth discussion of outdoor flooring materials, see p. 14.)

you could put up curtain walls using mosquito netting, semisheer or opaque fabric, or hemmed lightweight screening. On a deck, extend corner posts to make a place to string wire or hang curtains. On a recessed balcony, hang curtains from wire strung between both sides of the building. In the backyard, if you're lucky enough to have trees where you need them, you could run curtains between the trees on ropes.

Shelter from the storm (and sun)

If you want to maximize the use of your dining area and don't want to be driven inside by a light rain or have to restrict your party to the cool of the evening, plan for shelter in some form. Your site might provide its own shelter (trees nearby for shade and some rain protection). Otherwise, consider the strategic use of umbrellas, awnings, or canopies or site your dining area under an open-air structure.

UMBRELLAS

Aside from the shade of a tree, an umbrella is your least expensive option for providing shelter. Look for one that reflects the size and shape of your table or is only slightly larger—an umbrella that is much bigger (or smaller) than the table it shelters looks unbalanced. Standard sizes range from 7 ft. to 13 ft. in diameter. An umbrella that tilts has a distinct shade advantage, because you can angle it to block the harsh rays of the sun as it moves across the sky. An open umbrella can pose problems in heavy winds, often acting like a sail as it carries both itself and the table into a window or shrub. Try to get into the habit of closing your umbrella every evening and during storms.

A stand helps keep your umbrella upright. Even when the umbrella is inserted into a hole in a table, a stand further stabilizes it. The sturdier and heavier the stand, the better it works. I recommend heavy metal stands rather than plastic or water- or sand-filled arrangements, because their weight makes them more stable. Make sure the hole in the stand is the same size as your umbrella pole—there are lots of variations in pole diameters, and though you can sand down a too-big wooden pole, you can't modify a plastic one. (Holes in tables also vary, although they tend to be large, so it's rare to have a problem getting an umbrella pole to fit into a table.)

AWNINGS AND CANOPIES

Fabric awnings can also be used for shelter; they can be retractable (set on metal frames) or they are available in tentlike forms that cover all or part of a metal framework. Like a solid roof, awnings keep the rain out, but must be collapsed or removed at the end of the season in climates where it snows. Home stores offer inexpensive freestanding canopies on legs, which can be placed on any grassy or level surface.

ABOVE: An umbrella table casts a wide circle of shade on this dappled bluestone patio. Small trees planted along the edges offer more shade and add to a sense of enclosure.

FACING PAGE: An antique picket fence style is used here to mark the half-walls of the dining area. Even when the gate is open, this pergola feels like an enclosed room.

Weatherend® makes this custom 13-ft. round Umbrella Room, made of a wooden frame mounted on lolly columns grounded in concrete footings. The umbrella sits in the center and must be raised, opened, and resting on the framework for the roof to be rainproof.

gazebos or pavilions made to be homeowner assembled on a deck or directly on the lawn (these have no floor). They are often fitted with a weather-resistant canopy that hangs down. Remember that these kinds of side coverings can get warm in hot weather, so look for those that allow you to tie up the side walls, if desired.

A pergola is a completely open structure consisting of columns supporting overhead joists. Available from manufacturers in wood, vinyl, and steel requiring assembly,

Screen-wall tents are also an option for summer entertaining. These must also be collapsed and stored for winter.

PERMANENT OPEN-AIR STRUCTURES

A gazebo is a freestanding open structure with roof and floor and walls that only come up about waist high. They are available in wood and vinyl, and in a wide variety of styles (cedar roof shingles, elaborate gingerbread trim, screens, and windows) and sizes, from intimate to big enough to accommodate large parties. These structures can be delivered fully assembled, built on site, or shipped in kit form, but the homeowner is responsible for making sure the site is properly prepared (check with individual manufacturers about specifics). You can also buy open steel structures that serve as

Umbrella Tips

- The largest market umbrellas are rectangles that can be as big as 9 ft. by 11 ft. Although providing an enormous area of shade, they tend to be unstable in wind. If you buy such an umbrella, keep it closed when not in use.
- Make it a habit to collapse your umbrella before a wind- or rainstorm.
- If your folded umbrella gets thoroughly wet, open it at the first opportunity to let air in and sunshine kill any nascent mold.
- If the umbrella develops mold, first try leaving it open in bright sunlight. If that doesn't work, and if your umbrella is not a dark color, spray the affected areas with a diluted bleach solution. (Either dilute commercial bathroom tile spray 4 to 1 with plain water in a new squeeze bottle or make your own solution using 1 tbsp. to 3 tbsp. of bleach to 1 qt. of water.) Wait a minute or two, then hose down the umbrella well to completely remove the bleach, or it will develop holes. Leave open in the sun to dry. If your umbrella is dark, you'll have to rely on sunlight alone to kill any mold, as bleach will ruin it.
- Before storing your umbrella for the winter, brush it down with a broom to loosen any dirt or debris, or vacuum it. Store it, collapsed, in a dry place.

they can also be built from plans and kits.

For shade and shelter under a pergola, train fruit-bearing vines such as grapes or flowering vines like wisteria to grow up and over them. It may take a while, however, for the canopy to develop, depending on the particular vine planted. See p. 201 for more information on pergola planting.

When deciding what size structure to build or purchase, consider your entertaining needs; the last thing you want is to be crammed in tight at the table, with no room to push back your chairs. Also, take a good look at the architecture of the structure; many wooden pergolas are designed with overhangs, so, for example, a 16-ft.-square pergola would actually yield a 12-ft.-square space.

ABOVE: This pergola has been fitted with a light-filtering shade to form a canopy over the serene Asian-inspired dining area. Brick pavers, plants in containers, and soft square cushions for seating offer contrasting textures.

LEFT: A broadly striped, scalloped-edge awning shelters this dining area. The stripes on the chairs match the color but not the scale of the awning, making a pleasing variation on a theme.

every material at every price level, teak is always more expensive than a comparable metal or wicker set.

Putting furniture away for the season

Before storing your furniture for the season, inspect it. If it's dirty, give it a good wash while the hose is still connected. If it needs repair, try to do it before putting it away. Brush off all upholstery or vacuum it and put any cushions in a big cloth laundry bag or wrap them in an old sheet for protection. Avoid putting them in plastic bags, as mold can develop if the bag is airtight.

Store your furniture in a dry basement or garage, if you have the space. You can also purchase vinyl covers that fit over umbrellas, grills, sets of tables and chairs, and benches. These allow you to leave your furniture in place with the covers tied on. If you buy the best covers you can find, they should last a decade or so.

Outdoor Furniture

For leisurely dining in comfort, you'll want a sturdy weatherproof table and chairs. These are commonly sold as patio sets and come in a range of materials, from aluminum and plastic to teak and other tropical woods. Chairs with flexible seats (such as webbing), slings made of quick-drying fabrics, or those with optional cushions made of weather-resistant fabrics add comfort, although cushions can present a chore to move out and put away. Pay attention to the width and breadth of the seat of a chair (bigger is usually better) and whether or not you require chairs or tables to collapse for winter storage.

For a long-term investment, consider woods that age well, such as farmed teak, or metals not prone to rusting, such as aluminum. Although there are patio sets in

Setting the Stage for Entertaining

Because you are outdoors and less constrained by convention, you can do amazing things with your décor: Create a magical

How Much Space Do You Need to Sit?

An area at least 8 ft. by 8 ft. (or 64 sq. ft.) is a minimum requirement for a standard four-person square or round table. That's because you need room around the table and chairs for people to circulate. Keep in mind that you can have a long, narrow table to allow more seating in a more confined area.

No matter what size table you choose, allow space for people to move from the grill or yard to the table and at least 2 ft. to 3 ft. behind the chairs for passing space.

atmosphere with plants, candles, paper lanterns, or torches. Hang flags, pennants, wind chimes, or mobiles for color, motion, and sound. Don't be shy about mixing and matching colors and patterns. Outdoors, anything goes.

Outdoor tablecloths

Think about assembling a collection of tablecloths for outdoor use only. There are special cloths available for tables with umbrellas, with an opening for the umbrella pole or Velcro® seams for opening around the pole. Search remnant bins at fabric stores for long lengths of cloth, or use attractive bedsheets, cotton saris, or quilts to drape or wrap around your table. Oilcloth is another practical option and can be found

Outdoor Fabrics and Finishes

Acrylic fabrics: Woven from acrylic plastic, these fabrics are lightweight, resilient, quick drying, and resistant to sunlight, fading, soiling, stains, abrasion, and mildew. Acrylic fabrics look and feel like cotton, but are durable outdoors.

Vinyl and vinyl-coated polyester fabrics: These fabrics have an open mesh construction that allows air and water to pass through. They provide excellent resistance to abrasion, mildew, heat, stains, soiling, chemicals, fading, and sunlight.

Surface Finishes

Anodizing permanently seals the surface of aluminum, eliminating the formation of aluminum oxide.

Lacquer gives rattan and resin "wicker" furniture gloss and weather protection.

E-coating, used on iron and steel, forms a bond with the metal to inhibit rust and provide a base for powder coating.

Powder coating is a baked finishing process for aluminum, iron, and steel that produces a thick, durable, weather-resistant coating.

TOP LEFT: Farmed teak furniture offers durability and natural beauty. Because teak is an oily wood, it can withstand weather without splitting or cracking.

TOP RIGHT: Outdoor seating can be as soft, deep, and comfortable as indoor versions. Here, thick cushions provide comfort, yet can easily be whisked away if rain clouds threaten.

ABOVE: Indoor furniture can work outside if protected with exterior paint and brought under shelter out of season. Bright colors make a marvelous contrast to the green of lush foliage. The built-in bench that's part of the stucco wall provides seating on the other side of the table.

RIGHT: Looking remarkably light and airy, this metal dining set has lots of style. That lightness and the transparency of the tabletop help keep the furniture from dominating the patio and let the stone fireplace act as a focal point.

in patterned versions at fabric stores, or on the Internet at sites specializing in French tableware (*impermeable* is the French word for oilcloth).

Silverware and china

Disposable tableware is wonderfully convenient for eating outdoors, but using the real thing can transform the dining experience. Nothing is as elegant as fine linens and good china and glassware used out of doors; they add a sense of luxury and honor your guests.

Use odd pieces of secondhand silverware or purchase a set of outdoor flatware. Sets with bright-colored plastic handles are easy to find in the grass and are often so inexpensive that losing one is not a tragedy. Look for those that come in a caddy or stand or purchase one to keep them in.

Similarly, a sturdy set of plates, bowls, cups, and glasses made of enameled tin, melamine, or other colorful plastic can make outdoor dining both elegant and relaxed, because you need not fear their breaking. For space reasons, look for dishes that stack easily or are made to store in

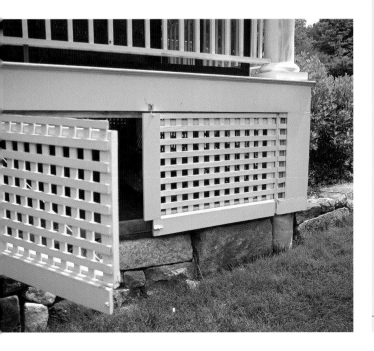

LEFT: Stacks of cushions are stored behind the wooden door in this stucco wall. The great advantage of this arrangement is that it's so close to the table.

BELOW: This clever homeowner hinged the lattice under his porch to create a storage area for outdoor furniture and equipment.

Outdoor Furniture Materials

Aluminum: Light and strong, it can't rust, but will show white aluminum oxide on its surface unless protected by paint or powder coating.

Iron: It's very heavy and durable and extremely strong, but will rust unless protected by paint or powder coating.

Plastic: Widely available and often inexpensive, molded plastic furniture is mass-produced and durable, and features integral color.

Wicker: Wicker furniture is made of various materials, and coated or treated to achieve varying degrees of weather impermeability. Choices include cellulose-covered stainless steel wires treated with resin and coated with polyester, fiberglass strands impregnated with resin, and woven vinyl or PVC. In addition, there's wicker or rattan, which is treated with a protective sealant and/or painted.

Wood: Look for furniture constructed from dense, oil-rich woods, which are naturally waterproof. Teak, mahogany, and jarrah are good examples of suitable farmed woods for outdoor furniture.

TOP RIGHT: These home-owners have set the stage for their party—South Asian in theme—with a scalloped tent, layers of patterned rugs, low Indian chairs, and pillows. The fountain in the pool provides restful music.

BOTTOM RIGHT: Patterned seat cushions on deep armchairs, colorful tableware, and a bright striped umbrella are at the ready for a great evening out of doors. Privacy is provided by the stockade fence and overgrown vine.

FACING PAGE: Masses of candles set the mood here, from the many candle tiers in the hanging chandelier to the rows of votive candles ranged along the fireplace mantle.

BELOW: Elegance out of doors is an easy accomplishment when you use fine china, bone-handled flatware, and hobnail glasses. Food always looks its best when presented amidst a neutral palette of whites, creams, and greens.

a container, so you can keep them in a convenient indoor or outdoor location. Thick-ribbed bistro glasses are exceptionally sturdy and stack easily, making them excellent outdoor candidates.

Candles and other live flame

Candles are a beautiful way to light an outdoor dining table and can be used in candle stands on the table, in clusters of small votive holders, or in hanging or standing chandeliers. Just be sure that the candles are sheltered from wind by glass, metal, or ceramic materials and not placed too close to anything that might combust, such as a curtain. Larger-scale illumination also packs a wallop—try using torches to set a festive mood. Luminaria, or candles set inside bags, can be placed along steps or paths to light the way. (For more on candles and other lighting possibilities, see p. 185.)

Social fire

Social fire refers to all the modern equivalents of gathering around a campfire or hearth. Somewhere in our DNA there must be a gene that attracts us to flickering flames, because sitting around a fire makes us feel good. Today we have a remarkable number of ways to keep those beguiling home fires burning in our own backyard.

FIRE PITS

Fire pits, which are usually shallow bowls often set on legs (so the surface underneath does not get too hot), are designed to be the central feature in a sitting area. They may be fueled with wood or gas (propane or natural gas) and may be strictly social or used for grilling as well. (Even when they are not set up for cooking, you can still roast marshmallows and make s'mores over a fire pit.)

Fire pits are constructed of metal, stone, or concrete and must be located in a well-ventilated area. If you are installing a gas-

Set on a fireproof surface, this portable wood-burning fire pit offers warmth and cheer. Candles in hurricane shades bring even more flicker to the circle of armchairs at dusk.

fueled fire pit, you'll need to plan for the gas line and make sure the gas outlet is located underneath the fire pit site. Although this is easy to do for an aboveground deck, it will require planning and a trench if installed at ground level.

Gas fire pits come in a variety of heights —from those that feel like campfires (on short legs a little above ground level), to coffee table or tabletop heights, up to fire pit tables at bar height for use with bar stools. These are all designed for conviviality, meant for people to sit in a circle around the flames. Models surrounded by table surfaces offer a place to set down a drink or plate of food while you talk, watch the fire dance in the center of the circle, and revel in the warmth on a cool evening.

One manufacturer makes a gas-fired campfire-log arrangement that can be put in

your own custom fire pit surround, whether that's a copper tub or a custom mosaic surround or even a circle of real boulders, for a completely convincing campfire. Gas fires like this put out considerable heat—as much as 60,000 BTUs to 75,000 BTUs per hour, depending on whether the fuel is propane or natural gas (natural gas is always hotter). Again, you'll need to run a gas line for this if you're interested in installing one.

Wood-fueled fire pits should come with a fire screen or spark guard surround that fits all around the opening—if it doesn't, buy one for safety's sake. The fire pit should be heavy enough so there is no danger that it can be blown or knocked over when in use.

As with any live fire, keep an eye on your fire pit at all times, keep fire extinguishing supplies handy, and place it on a fireproof hearth pad.

CHIMINEAS

A chiminea is a freestanding, portable open fireplace. Originally made of ceramic materials, they are now sold in cast aluminum and cast iron as well, and are fueled either by wood or gas. When fueled by gas, chimineas can use either LP or natural gas, with the fuel accessed through a natural-gas line or via an LP cylinder. All chimineas, no matter

how they are fueled, look rather like a small igloo with a tall chimney and short legs.

Each of the chiminea materials has its advantages and disadvantages. Clay versions are inexpensive, but fragile and subject to breakage and thermal shock—that means you need to heat up a clay chiminea slowly and lay the logs in gently. If you choose such a version, look for the thickest, heaviest model for durability and be aware that some people find them frustrating to keep alight because many do not draw well and require constant feeding of kindling to stay lit. Further, you need to protect clay chimineas from cold weather and freezing.

Cast iron is a beautiful material, but rusts over time when exposed to damp. It's also brittle, so it can break if it's dropped or knocked into heavily. However, cast iron chimineas can be extremely attractive and sturdy, lasting for many years if properly

cared for. Cast iron chimineas weigh significantly more than those constructed of other materials, making them, essentially, permanent fixtures.

Beyond Citronella: Keeping Mosquitoes at Bay

There are a number of new anti-insect machines on the market in addition to those familiar bug zappers. The newest generation of insect-prevention technology uses puffs of body-temperature CO_2 (what humans exhale), lures, and lights to attract bugs. Designed primarily for mosquitoes, these machines suck the bugs in and trap them. They are fueled by gas cylinders and are sold scaled to the size of your yard, ranging from half an acre to more than an acre.

Portable propane-powered mosquito lures like this one are effective because they use puffs of CO_2 and pheromones to attract mosquitoes and then trap them.

Perched on a cement wall capped by a terra-cotta tile, this chiminea creates a focal point even when not in use. When it's lit, the dancing flames are at just the right height for contemplation.

Cast aluminum is durable, unlikely to rust, and strong without great weight, making it easy to move.

When buying a wood-burning chiminea, look for a large or medium-size model, so you can use standard-size logs. Do note that most dealers offer gas conversion kits for LP, or gel inserts, which function like Sterno® cans. Make sure the chimney is tall and open so that it will draw air efficiently. When burning properly, there should only be smoke at the start of the fire and at the end. Chimineas are meant to be bottom heavy so they won't tip over; check models you are considering to make sure this is the case. Because sparks can start fires, buy a fire screen for your wood-burning chiminea as well as a cover to protect it from weather. (Gas-fueled models don't spark.) No matter what your chiminea is made of, but particularly with a clay model, place a heatproof surface such as a hearth pad, ceramic or stone tile, or cement board under it when using it on a wooden deck.

Fire Safety

With any open fire, keep a fire extinguisher handy. Be sure all gas tanks are at least 3 ft. away from an open flame and that all open flames have fire screens. Never place a heat-generating appliance closer than 3 ft. to any combustible surface, whether upholstered furniture, the side of your house, or a wooden chair. Never leave a fire (whether candle or campfire) unattended.

FIREPLACES

Fireplaces are one of the hottest (no pun intended) backyard objects of desire because they add such tremendous appeal to an outdoor room. Think about sitting on an outdoor couch facing a fireplace or lounging in a hot tub while watching dancing flames, or imagine dining under the stars with a fireplace that warms your back on a cold night, and you will immediately understand the appeal.

Further, fireplaces bring families and friends together as they literally gather around the hearth. When the fireplace is outside, it adds wow power because it's both informal and unexpected. You can even cook in your wood-burning fireplace—see William Rubel's book *The Magic of Fire*, or go to his website (www.williamrubel.com) for recipes. Fireplaces can be surprisingly versatile to cook in—in addition to a Tuscan grill (which fits over the coals in a fireplace), you can roast on a spit or bake in a clay cloche buried in the embers.

Alternatively, new outdoor gas fireplaces offer flames without smoke (or chimneys) and come with different heat capacities so they can be customized for your climate. Designed with weatherproof glass doors and top vents to direct heat forward, such fireplaces, like wood-burning models, generate warmth that allows you to extend the season of outdoor rooms. (See p. 154 for a discussion of patio heaters, which offer warmth without visible fire.)

Where you locate an outdoor fireplace depends first on how it is fueled. A wood-burning fireplace requires a chimney and, if located away from the house (in the garden, for instance), must have a chimney tall enough to clear the roof of the closest building.

Alternatively, you could build a fireplace onto your house or porch, but again, the chimney must project well above the roof-line, for safety's sake. Be aware too that if you live in an area with heavy snow, a chim-

ney located at the low end of a steep roof (even a brick one) can be swept away by the weight of melting snow. It is always safer to locate a chimney along the gable end of a building, or high up near the ridgeline of a sloped roof. Check with your fire department and the local building code for the rules and regulations regarding chimneys, which may vary according to location and in relation to the materials of your roof.

Indoor/outdoor fireplaces, those built to open in two directions (for example, outdoors onto a porch and indoors onto a family room), share a common chimney (if wood-burning) and do not have an internal divider. This is one of the biggest trends today in the hearth world, because it allows you to enjoy a fire from inside or outside the house. When the fireplace is not in use, a glass screen or cover keeps the outside out and the inside in.

Carved out of desert sandstone, this dramatic fireplace is one-of-a-kind. Because the fire is at eye level to a seated person, it has extraordinary presence.

Gas fireplaces are much easier to site, because their requirements are less challenging. They are made to be installed against noncombustible surfaces such as concrete block, or with clearances so as not to touch combustible surrounds such as wooden studs. A gas-fired fireplace doesn't need a chimney; it vents its heat toward the viewer or upward or to the rear, depending on the model. You can choose such fireplaces with the maximum heat/BTU output you desire in many sizes, styles, and configurations (from corner fireplaces to freestanding to those inset into walls). They come with glass windows to view the fire, and some models offer fire-screen door kits for an even more realistic look. They all feature faux logs made of a ceramic material; some offer interior bricks with a smoked finish. Although these fireplaces are fueled by gas, they require an electrical hookup to power the fan that sends the heat toward you. The fire is controlled by a switch or a remote control, and can be set at different levels of flame and heat. Again, you'll need to plan for running gas and electrical lines.

Patio heaters

Even in southern California, summer evenings can have a chill. To enjoy the outdoors on such nights, and to extend the season of use, manufacturers have created patio heaters to provide a circle of warmth. These heaters come in essentially two styles: an LP gas-fueled omnidirectional large lamppost model based on those used on restaurant

A long table set in front of a fireplace under a sheltering roof sets the scene for many dinners with family and friends. The candles in the hanging chandelier offer overhead lighting, and the fireplace built into the side wall of the house offers warmth.

miniaturized tabletop model that puts out between 11,000 BTUs and 14,000 BTUs.

You'll see, as you begin to shop for heaters, that each comes with descriptions of their "heat shadow," or range of heat dispersal. Large standing heaters generally heat about a 20-ft. circle, whereas tabletop heaters claim up to a 10-ft. diameter. A tabletop heater will be adequate for guests seated around a circular or square table, at least heating their faces and the fronts of their bodies. To heat the backs of those diners, you would also need to place a couple

LEFT: Minimalist style can look great out of doors. This modern unadorned fireplace makes a bold statement, especially when paired with the long table and red chairs.

BELOW: A freestanding fireplace anchors one end of this living room pavilion, where it is located just beyond the roofline. Two auxiliary heaters are mounted on the ceiling.

terraces, which sheds heat in a circle, and a powerful electric wall-mounted box style, which aims heat in one direction. Both styles are effective and your choice should be based on what will work best for you.

For example, on a deck or patio without walls or a roof, a post-style heater, set in the middle of the space, will create a comfort zone for a number of people seated nearby. Most of these put out about 40,000 BTUs. Available in different colors or stainless steel, these heaters can be portable or permanently set in concrete; they hide a 20-lb. LP tank in their base, which provides about ten hours of heat per load. There is also a

RIGHT: This massive stone fireplace is visible from inside the house as well as out.

BOTTOM RIGHT: Tucked above the beams that tie this porch together, an electric heater aims warmth down toward seated diners.

FACING PAGE TOP: Attached to the overhead trellis, this heater aims heat down to the table.

FACING PAGE BOTTOM: What better place is there to enjoy the pleasures of the table than a little neoclassical garden temple devoted to food? This sheltered dining room overlooks gardens and a broad patio.

of large post-style heaters behind them on all four sides of your seating area.

For a large open deck, patio, or garden, a number of large post-style heaters can be set in a grid to create overlapping circles of warmth, raising the temperature 10° to 25°. All large portable post heaters are built with an automatic safety switch that turns them off if they are tilted or knocked over. They should never be used on a screened porch, as they are made for real outdoor use only.

Although at least one electric patio heater is available in the same tall post style as the gas models, most electric models are single-directional, much smaller, and use ordinary household current. Solaire makes a wall-mounted heater that can put out enough heat to warm 96 sq. ft. Because it is electric, it can be used on screened porches and in outdoor spaces that have roofs, but it is also

rated for completely outdoor use. It's energy efficient, puts out immediate heat without a warm-up period, and costs about 11 cents an hour to use.

All in all, the point of an outdoor dining space is pleasure—the pleasure of good company, the pleasures of the table, and the pleasures of the great outdoors. As you create a comfortable place to talk and eat, a place you can decorate with imagination or make magical with lighting or cozy with warmth, keep in mind that it's all in aid of conviviality—your nearest and dearest are there to have a wonderful evening with you in the great outdoors.

Italy in Texas

Gary Peese and James David, partners in Gardens, a unique shop in Austin (www.gardens-austin.com), spend much of their leisure time in their own garden. Because David is a landscape architect and Peese is a plantsman and avid cook, their home gardens function as a laboratory for trying out designs, plants, and products. Their motto is simplicity plus elegance, and those ideas are central to the outdoor spaces they have made.

ABOVE: Grilling pineapple slices and shrimp at the same time creates sweet smoke and an appetizing hors d'oeuvre.

LEFT: A long table framed by stonework and surrounded by 10 red Swedish indoor/outdoor rubber chairs shows the owners' signature mix of lighthearted exuberance and strong design. Pavers laid in a herringbone pattern form a rug for the table, whereas the masonry pyramid and stone sphere mark the wall between the dining space and the wood-fired cooking area.

RIGHT: On the other side of the wall from the patio dining area are three wood-fired barbecues: The smoker is on the far right, the middle grill is used for cooking for crowds, and the Tuscan grill on the left is most useful for small events.

BELOW: Here a leg of lamb cooks *à la ficelle* (on a string) in the fireplace on the back porch off the indoor kitchen. The garlic-studded meat spins in front of the fire and drips into a casserole of potatoes raised up on inverted plant pots. Cooking meat on a string is an ancient culinary method that delivers uncommon flavor. Rosemary branches are used for basting the meat as it cooks.

On the steep land around their home, David and Peese have created a series of dining, cooking, and garden spaces that highlight their love of Italy. Stone retaining walls form the boundaries of different garden rooms, an artful water feature reflects the sky, and Mediterranean plants in large Italian pots mark transitional spaces and form focal points. At dusk, twinkling lights strung between trees transform the patio dining area into a Texas version of a party in the piazza. It is a place to eat, to dream, and to enjoy the company of others.

To that end, there is a wood-fired pizza oven, a back porch eating area with a fireplace that's also used for cooking, a long dining table set on its own long patio near a triple set of wood-fired cookers, as well as numerous garden spots for sitting, talking, and enjoying vistas. In addition, there's a kitchen garden filled with heirloom plants and unusual European varieties of herbs and vegetables, as well as a thriving exotic chicken population that supplies eggs for the table. All in all, this Texas version of *la dolce vita* is a great example of outdoor living.

This back porch just off the indoor kitchen is the site of a fireplace and sheltered dining area, used both for intimate meals and drinks before dinner. The fireplace holds a Tuscan grill for cooking.

ABOVE: On the other side of the porch table and fireplace, a stainless steel gas grill offers quick and easy cooking. It's set into a cabinet that also holds an undercounter refrigerator and storage and workspace.

RIGHT: Antique and traditional French crockery are used to hold cooking tools.

FACING PAGE: A limestone-faced Italian wood-fired oven is used for pizza and high-heat roasting. Fresh herbs from the garden enhance the flavors of the pizzas. The cavity above the oven is used to hold baking dishes, platters, and crocks, the space below for fuel.

Every garden needs artful meditation space. Here, in the approach to the dining patio, gravel and flagstones are combined to frame a stone sculpture. Plants clipped into spheres provide form, and the oversize Italian pot adds scale. Overhead, strings of piazza lights add their festive glow.

Maine Screen House and Garden

Jonathan King and Jim Stott are the founders of Stonewall Kitchen in York, Maine. Like their products and shops, their home and garden reflect their passion for good food, casual living with flair, and great design. Off the interior kitchen of their home, they've created a series of extraordinary outdoor living areas that move seamlessly from the garden, to the pool, to the freestanding screen house dining room

ABOVE: You can cook lots of food on a big portable grill, using both levels and the side burner. Inside the screen house, to the left of the table, is a sitting area. Outdoor copper lighting fixtures add warm tones to this cool climate.

LEFT: Looking across the pool, the screen house anchors that end of the outdoor living space. Chaise longues offer poolside seating. The small outdoor dining table and chairs on the pool patio are an alternative spot for a meal or a snack for those who want to sit in the sun. The door leading to the indoor kitchen is to the right, under the pergola.

and living room. Because they do all their food prep work in the home's indoor kitchen, their outdoor kitchen consists solely of a portable gas grill. Unlike having a fixed kitchen, there's never a problem with smoke in the screen house or near the chaise longues on the pool patio because the grill is easy to move out of the way, even while food is cooking.

Jonathan works side by side in the design and care of all the gardens with his landscape architect, Jacquelyn Nooney. The gardens consist of box-edged parterres and rectangular beds divided by stone-edged gravel paths. They display an amazing diversity of color and texture, combining both ornamentals and vegetables.

Vine-covered pergolas planted with clem-atis and wisteria line two sides of the garden and an English greenhouse/conservatory provides a place to start plants from seed, offering these North Country gardeners a way to extend the season. The small patio outside the conservatory is used as another dining place. Near the conservatory, a picket fence opens onto the vegetable garden of raised beds filled with all manner of heirloom vegetables and flowers for the table.

The screen house, located at one end of the pool not far from the indoor kitchen, has a teak table that can seat six to eight people and a sitting area. Its heavy mahogany doors glide easily on tracks that line up with the screen walls so that the screen house can function like an open pavilion or be closed off to protect guests from insects.

Boxwood-edged parterres border the house. The kitchen door is visible on the right, marked by green shutters and antique metal lights.

ABOVE: The greenhouse/conservatory comes from England; the patio in front of it is used for alfresco meals. In summer, a potted bay tree flourishes on the stone wall. Masses of cannas add a tropical touch.

LEFT: Dining on the greenhouse patio, the air is filled with the scent of bay leaves. Entertaining on the Maine coast is easy when fresh salmon, asparagus tied with a chive from the garden, and bread from a local bakery are on the menu.

ABOVE: Inside the screen house, cream-painted bead-board creates coziness, and Arts and Crafts style light fixtures add another level of detail. The building's mix of transparent screen walls and subtly colored painted wood allows visitors to feel protected from the elements, yet still in the garden.

RIGHT: Behind the picket fence, heirloom vegetables grow in raised beds. Beyond the large vegetable garden, a stretch of woods offers protection from the wind.

FACING PAGE: Mass planting is one of the secrets of this garden's success, especially because the choices of materials are so sensitive to both color and texture. Here, chard, chives, and thyme make a vivid contrast to the beds planted with echinacea, coreopsis, and astilbe behind them.

At night, low-voltage lighting in the pergola canopy makes the flowers in the garden pop. Line-voltage lights on either side of the kitchen door create large pools of intense illumination, pointing the way back into the house.

Hidden Courtyard, Poolside Kitchen

In sight of the Golden Gate Bridge in Marin County, Dan and Lisa Weiss's hilltop dining patio and promontory seating area have fabulous long-distance views. On the other side of the house, in an inner courtyard, their pool and poolside outdoor kitchen are all about closeness and scale. Dan, a premium house builder, and Lisa, a cookbook author, met in art school. Their fine eye for detail and perfect

ABOVE: The same scene at night shows how lighting enhances the whole experience: Downlights fitted into the canopy of the oven and over the grill and counter offer ample illumination for cooking tasks. Uplight sconces along the walls of the house provide ambient light, whereas the pool lighting provides atmosphere. Candles along the length of the table softly illuminate food and guests.

LEFT: Looking across the pool, the outdoor kitchen is all in one line and features a wood-burning oven and charcoal grill. Because the outdoor kitchen is so close to the house, a refrigerator and sink were unnecessary. The long teak table can seat 14 people.

ABOVE: Storage under the pigmented concrete counter next to the gas grill holds a terra-cotta pot used for roasting in the wood oven. A stainless steel door protects the interior.

RIGHT: The pool room looks across the pool to the outdoor kitchen. The mosaic tile floor adds pattern and detail, complementing the texture of the seagrass chairs indoors and weathered teak chairs outside.

FACING PAGE: Wood-fired pizza gets more flavor from fresh rosemary, heirloom tomatoes, and basil.

placement is apparent everywhere you look. From the big indoor kitchen to the landscaping, which both reveals and enhances so many of the outdoor spaces, this is a home where the visual is paramount.

It's also a place where fine cooking is a given, and great recipes are tested almost nightly. Lisa is known as an outstanding chef-collaborator, and she has made a specialty of writing cookbooks with notable Bay Area restaurant chefs. This means that both the indoor and outdoor kitchens function as test kitchens, as she cooks restaurant-quality recipes scaled down for household use. Dan has built both kitchens to work professionally as well as for family use, enlisting the advice of the many chefs they cherish as friends. The wood-burning oven in the outdoor kitchen is a case in point: Dan designed it with advice

from chef Mark Franz of San Francisco's Farallon restaurant.

The pool courtyard is formed by two masonry walls faced with stone and covered with ivy that separate the property from the street and a neighbor, and by two of the house's walls—one formed by the kitchen and the other by the pool room and the back of the garage. The garage's rear wall has an innovative element: an additional set of roll-up doors on its back wall facing the pool, making it possible to use the empty garage as a roofed pavilion for parties. Next to it, the house's pool room sports a patterned mosaic floor that's impervious to chlorine, and the outdoor patio's floor is concrete. Around the corner, forming the fourth side of the courtyard, the kitchen wall is glass, making it easy to check on the progress of what's cooking outside.

Off the opposite side of the indoor kitchen, several dining and sitting areas take advantage of the views. Near the house, a round umbrella table and chairs provide convenient seating. At the edge of the garden, on the promontory, armchairs and a side table offer the perfect place to watch the sun set over the bay.

Promontory seating offers a beautiful bay view and the perfect place to track clouds and sunsets.

FACING PAGE: This dining area is just off the bay side of the kitchen and simultaneously offers views and a sense of enclosure, thanks to the hedges of lavender and rosemary that crisscross the garden.

LEFT: A cast concrete table offers stability in what is often a windy spot.

BELOW LEFT: Black and white dishes and black and white textiles lend elegance to a simple table.

BELOW RIGHT: The Bay Area is famous for its farmers' markets, and these heirloom tomatoes are a good example of the range of Pacific plenty.

Grace Notes:
Lighting, Sound Systems, Planting, and Water Features

Here, you'll find the grace notes, ornamentation, and harmonies that make the outdoor experience sweeter. Each of these important elements adds flourishes to your outdoor space, as well as comfort and beauty, and together they can help to make the difference between a space you love to use and one that you don't.

Exterior lighting and thoughtful planting can enhance the appearance of an outdoor kitchen, dining area, and entertainment area, highlighting desirable features and hiding those that are less so. Lighting increases the safety of after-dark use and can create magical effects, whereas planting helps to define the boundaries of a space and beautify the area. We'll first look at wired systems— lighting and sound—then go on to planting and water features.

FACING PAGE: Semi-enclosed patios like this are close enough to the house to easily make electrical connections. Pendant lights hang from the vine-covered pergola rafters, whereas other plantings climb the lattice walls for privacy.

ABOVE: Honeysuckle twined around a post makes an emphatic backdrop for this garden fountain, and distracts us from the fence and close-by neighbor's house.

Electricity in the Outdoor Kitchen

Electrical landscape lighting generally runs in a connected series of fixtures. The most common outdoor lighting systems are low voltage, which offer efficiency and energy savings by stepping down house power. In contrast, commercial or large-scale landscaping lighting systems use line power, running on full house current.

Line power systems are made for areas where brilliant light may be required, including security lighting or lighting at some great distance (for example, trees in the landscape), where the power requirements would overwhelm a low-voltage system. Because such systems require more complex planning and are potentially dangerous if installed incorrectly, an electrical contractor should plan and install them.

Low-voltage systems are the most popular electric landscape lighting option, because, in addition to their other virtues, they are easy to install and effective. They work by stepping electrical house power of 110v down to 12v via a transformer, which is mounted inconspicuously on an exterior wall and connected to an outdoor GFCI (ground fault circuit interrupter) outlet. The size of the transformer needs to match the number, distance, and wattage of the fixtures you choose, both because there are limits to how much power a transformer can handle and because a line loses power over distance (this is called "voltage drop"). Consequently, complex lighting plans require a number of transformers to work properly and should be planned with the help of a knowledgeable dealer or lighting expert. These days, professional or high-quality low-voltage landscape lighting can fulfill almost the same range of lighting tasks as a line-voltage system, both in terms of power and design flexibility. And thanks

In the foreground, two landscape lights (on either side of the path) illuminate the steps. Lights on the patio show the way to the house (on right) and to the path up the hill (center), where the gardens are lit to show off the dramatic shapes of plants.

are run in trenches about 6 in. underground between your home's electrical circuit box and the outdoor kitchen. Make sure to keep track of their paths so you don't hit them when digging a hole.

Lighting the Way into and around the Outdoor Kitchen

Every outdoor kitchen will need to have a baseline of general illumination to subtly light a whole area such as a patio or a deck. An easy to way to think about this basic level of light is to imagine it as the outdoor equivalent of a nightlight—it lights the room at a low level and enables you to find your way. A deck lighting plan that illustrates this is a series of low-voltage bollard lights mounted on the upright posts of a deck's railing. Area lighting is often augmented with specialized lighting for specific tasks or accents.

Lighting stairs and paths

Access lights, such as recessed stair lights, a series of small umbrella or pagoda-shaped lights along the pathway from house to kitchen, or wall-hung entry lights that point the way back to the door of the house,

If stone steps such as these are to be traversed at night, careful lighting is a must. The lanterns shown here are enough to show the change of level, but not enough for safe travel.

to the variety of bulbs available, it can do this at a lower running cost. Good lighting fixtures may be more expensive than you expect, but will prove their worth in long, trouble-free use. Low-voltage systems are available for DIY installation in kit form; however, it is always a prudent idea to consult with an expert before proceeding.

All electric lights used outdoors must be approved for outdoor use, as they will be exposed to damp and temperature extremes. Make sure to choose electric fixtures, switches, and plugs that are specifically UL-approved for outdoor installation and that all outlets are fitted with GFCIs (which prevent electric shock and short circuits by switching off if they get wet).

For all outdoor electrical requirements, weatherproof cable is used and often housed in PVC pipes for further protection. These

Designing a Lighting Plan

Lighting designers are the professionals who create light plans; your garden designer or landscape architect may also be qualified. Many high-end lighting dealers will be glad to consult with you on your light plan and may offer design services as part of their package. Use them, if possible, to get as much bang for your buck as you can. Buying lighting is expensive and it can also be pricey to install. It makes sense to plan with intelligence so your money is well spent. All complex electrical lighting, particularly line-voltage systems, should be installed by a qualified electrician and must conform to local zoning, if applicable. In addition to an electrician, you will need a landscaper or contractor to dig trenches for electrical cables, or you'll need to do this yourself.

All about Access Lights

Outdoor access lights are the most widely available outdoor lights, are sold as "landscape lighting," and are available in a wide range of styles, from modern to traditional. Most of them run on a low-voltage system off a weatherproof cable that runs underground in a shallow trench, feeding off a remote transformer that connects to an exterior outlet. Typically, path fixtures have a stake at the bottom and are pushed into position. The power and number of fixtures determine the size of the transformer and the maximum length of the cable, and many retailers sell these in sets to make installation easy. Such path lights often take the form of a mushroom or pagoda canopy or lantern on top of a short pole, and are designed to shed a small pool of light. Similar fixtures are made to be mounted on deck posts or tall lantern posts. In contrast, recessed stair lights, which are designed to shed light across the steps or risers, offer less illumination and are built flush into the sides of wooden, stone, or concrete steps during their construction, so if these are of interest, you've got to plan ahead for them.

recessed, plan ahead, as you'll need to know the dimensions and electrical requirements of the lights before the actual structure of the kitchen or grill counter or island is built.

One kind of light made expressly for outdoor cooking is a small surface-mounted spotlight that clamps onto a grill, and some grill manufacturers provide such headlights as standard features. Another kind of task light is a floor lamp or wall fixture used on a screened porch for reading light. Because screened porches and buildings like gazebos are the most protected of outdoor spaces, outdoor-rated pendant lights can also be used, to illuminate a dining table, for example.

RIGHT: Some grills feature an integral light for cooking after dusk.

show people the route to take when dining outdoors or coming back inside the house. They serve as navigational aids to your guests, and are particularly important if your outdoor kitchen is located away from the house and stairs must be negotiated. These lights are available in a wide range of fixtures in low-voltage and solar versions and offer different levels of illumination based on their power and, in the case of low voltage, their bulb type. They are the outdoor equivalent of hallway lighting.

Task light to work by

Task lighting is designed to make doing a job easier by providing a high level of light focused on a work surface, like under-cabinet lights shining onto the counter in an indoor kitchen. In an outdoor kitchen with a roof, fixtures mounted on beams can be aimed down at the counters. Built-in grills can have lights recessed or surface mounted within or on the stone or brickwork, much like step lights. Again, if you want the lights

LEFT: Down spots make pools of light on this terrace, illuminating the dining area in the foreground and the sitting area behind. The fire provides even more light and glow. A light aimed up at the foliage of the shrub on the left softens the hard edges of the darkness beyond.

BELOW: For low-level illumination and a touch of whimsy, twist rope lights up the umbrella's support.

Manipulating light for function and visual effect

Lighting can add a theatrical element to the view from outdoor rooms, drawing the eye toward different features and obscuring others. For example, once you're seated at the table, you probably won't want to see the cooking area. Separately switched lights allow you to illuminate one area while sending the other into shadow.

The best lighting is always the most natural looking, with a subtle light source and sensitive placement in relation to architecture, people, and objects. In other words, make the light the main event, not the fixture. Here are some classic ways to manipulate light for effect:

Downlighting is used in an outdoor kitchen to spotlight cooking areas—the light shines down from above onto a surface. A downlight can be a central ceiling fixture like a big lantern, but more comfortable light with less glare can usually be accom-

plished by setting downlights judiciously. In an indoor kitchen, such lights are usually arranged in a 2-ft. or 3-ft. grid along the ceiling in recessed can fixtures to create illumination without shadows. Outdoors we seldom require that degree of constant light, so set downlights only where needed to illuminate work areas, taking care to aim them at the counter in such a way as to

next to the house or a garden wall or fence.

Uplighting can illuminate the roof or ceiling of your outdoor kitchen or entertaining area, much like the sun makes clouds radiant with light. Creating soft light shining upward where a wall or post meets the roof or ceiling provides comfortable ambient light, because the light bounces off the surface and reflects down. One subtle way to do this in an outdoor room or under an umbrella is to use a string of lights, like outdoor Christmas lights. For a permanent installation, use commercial rope lighting under the inner eaves of a roof, making the ceiling lift and glow.

prevent shadows when people stand at the grill, sink, or wood-burning oven. When possible, these lights should be located well above you, aimed at the work surface, not behind you.

If you need to illuminate a grill that is out in the open and not under a roof, downlights can be mounted on nearby trees or a post, or wall-mounted if the grill is located

USING LIGHT TO HIGHLIGHT A FOCAL POINT

All of these light techniques can create the outdoor equivalent of a great painting hung opposite the dining table or the couch; they give you and your guests something beautiful to look at as you relax and talk together.

Wall-washing or *grazing* is the technique of brushing or even flooding a surface with light (depending on the fixture, position, and wattage). You can use this technique to dramatic effect, for example, to illuminate a rough stone wall, intensifying your perception of its irregularity and texture. Typically, such fixtures are small low-voltage halogen lamps angled back at the wall from 6 in. to 8 in. away.

Accent lighting can be used to make a focal point of the front face of a wood-fired oven, a tree, or a display of flowers. These lights can be up, down, wall-washing, or cross-lights, but their purpose is always to enhance display and perception.

Put something in the spotlight with *spot* or *task lighting*, either for display (such as pointing to a feature) or to light up a work area.

Beware of Too Much Light!

Homeowners need to consider the effect the light they build into their outdoor spaces may have on neighbors. It is always a good idea to err on the side of too little rather than too much when choosing the wattage or intensity of light. The least-light-polluting fixtures are hooded and closely aimed, so the light they spill is controlled. It's important to remember that a little light goes a very long way out of doors, so choose fixtures with the lowest possible wattages for the job.

MAKING THE OUTDOORS MAGIC WITH LIGHT

Think of these lighting techniques as creating eye appeal that you can enjoy from the leisure of your outdoor dining area—great visual effects that can only happen at night, out of doors.

Mirror a sculpture—set up a light on the far side of a water feature so that an object is mirrored in the water when seen from the patio or other spot in your outdoor kitchen. To work, the object has to be well lit and the water must be dark. If you've included a large water feature in your plan, this is one technique you won't want to miss.

Silhouette a plant by backlighting it against a garden wall. The plant shows up as a bold silhouette against the textured surface of the background. A related kind of lighting is called a *halo effect*, created by backlighting and slightly cross-lighting a tree without using a background feature to shadow the form against. *Shadowing* uses a small light to the side and lower front of a feature to cast a shadow (of a plant, statue, or water feature) against a wall without throwing the object into clear silhouette. All of these are extremely useful ways of creating a nighttime focal point.

Simulating moonlight is perhaps the most magical of light effects, achieved by mounting low-powered lights in trees or on surrounding walls or garden features to wash the trunks and lower foliage with light. It is often done with an accompanying low-level uplight at ground level to anchor the tree.

Lights mounted in the trees simulate moonlight in this romantic installation on the water. The lantern at right marks a path.

RIGHT: Fire light, electric light, and candles all combine to illuminate this patio. Small candles in tall candelabras decorate the table. The overhead light mounted on the fan provides the strongest illumination, and functions to make a baseline of visibility at night.

BELOW: A large pillar candle burns for hours without harm, thanks to the noncombustible heavy metal lantern.

This is a more complicated setup to tackle, but it's a very powerful lighting effect that's worth attempting if you'd like a "wow" response to your outdoor kitchen.

Cross-lighting is a way of lighting something from the side, illuminating its texture and form in a more indirect fashion. It's extremely effective for objects like statues, as well as on steps and/or risers. If you've got a garden sculpture or a dramatic rock outcrop, try this technique to make it really pop at night.

Alternatives to Electric Illumination

Electricity isn't the only way to get the lighting you want. Here are some alternatives.

Natural gas: In areas with natural gas, outdoor lighting fixtures are available for that fuel in a wide variety of styles.

Solar lights: These use photovoltaic cells to generate light from energy stored from the sun during the day. Their exact level of power depends on the amount of light

they are exposed to, as well as the power and efficiency of the battery, although it is always low level. Usually inexpensive, they are widely available as spike-bottomed path lights (usually sold in packs of four or six to line a walkway between the house and the outdoor kitchen). In addition, you can buy solar-powered security lights and deck lighting systems attached to remote solar collectors. They do not require wiring or trenches and can even be placed in a shady area that gets some natural light. They go on automatically as it gets darker and cannot be turned on or off. If you want to turn them off, you'll have to pull them out of the ground and put them away.

Live fire: Live fire in the form of luminaria (candles set in open paper bags partially filled with sand to stabilize them) or masses of tea lights can accent the outdoor kitchen and the walk to it in great style. Dining tables can be lit by candle chandeliers hung from an overhead trellis or a tree branch, or the dining area can be surrounded by tiki torches. The kitchen counter can be lit by pillar candles in hurricane shades, kerosene

lanterns, or strings of lanterns, along with the flicker of live fire from a fireplace or masonry oven.

Using electricity doesn't preclude using any of these more atmospheric non-electric options—you can easily mix and match different kinds of light to create different moods.

Outdoor Sound

Because it makes sense to consider all wiring at the same time, you should decide whether you want to wire your outdoor kitchen for sound when planning your electrical system. Although some people may feel that the only sound that belongs outside is birdsong, others will want sound systems to enhance their outdoor rooms.

Like light, sound creates ambiance and adds flavor to the sensual mix of outdoor pursuits. You can choose to have sound only in the outdoor kitchen, or on the deck or patio, or by the pool or hot tub, or everywhere in the yard. What your needs are will determine, in large part, what kinds of equipment are suitable, but bear in mind that the easiest backyard sound system you can devise will be limited in scope to produce optimal sound quality.

Every sound expert I spoke to recommends that consumers get knowledgeable help to plan their outdoor systems. Such help is available from authorized dealers (usually at no additional cost), or from sound consultants or contractors (who may mark up prices). No matter whom you consult, your musical preferences and the characteristics of your site will determine what you need for optimal outdoor sound. Although DIY-ers can install a system themselves, most experts caution against this and suggest that you hire the dealer or someone they recommend to do the installation.

Using Candle Power with Abandon

When I lived in Denmark for two years, I learned to use candles in ways I never had before. Because the Scandinavian winter is so long and so dark (the opposite of summer's midnight sun is winter's midday dusk), Danes use the flicker of candles to cheer themselves. Now that I'm back in this country, I use candles to light the way through our less-than-midnight-sun summer nights. I put tea lights and candles that I buy in bulk in the bottom of drinking glasses (so there's no danger of fire) and line pathways with them, set them on stone walls, and place them on the ground to edge the patios. Candles go in hanging lanterns made of washed tin cans pierced with nail holes or can openers and threaded with wire for hanging, or I arrange the lanterns on the floor along the edges of the deck. When I set a long table outdoors, I put a tea light at each place, often in a little glass holder, so that the table has a center strip of flickering, soft light. If it's a really festive occasion and the weather isn't too hot, I freeze ice and fresh blossoms in empty milk cartons until the outside shell is frozen but the inside is still slushy. I pour out the slush and water in the center, peel off the carton, and have a beautiful rectangular ice candle holder. I put a taper in the center and the light silhouettes the shape of the flowers frozen in the ice. Set in saucers along the table, these ephemeral candle holders add magic and bits of welcome chill to a long summer evening's delight.

Small votive candles set in glass containers line the table and mark each place. The large pillar candle protected by the glass hurricane shade lights the center. To prevent guttering and uneven drips, it's always a good idea to protect flames with glass surrounds.

To understand outdoor sound systems, a little technical know-how is necessary: Sound that travels from a speaker to your ear is called "direct sound." When this happens inside a home, the sound actually becomes less direct, as it bounces off walls, ceiling, furnishings, and rugs, all of which may absorb or, more likely, reflect some of that sound, generally making it seem louder and richer. Because this doesn't happen outside, all sound out of doors seems less loud and less dimensional because it is dispersed. For that reason an outdoor system needs to be more powerful and more efficient than an indoor system. Besides sounding weak, outdoor sound can suffer from an echo, especially when speakers are placed too far apart; in that case the sound can reach your ears separately, with a delay. For outdoor sound systems to work well, the speakers must be highly efficient and produce a loud acoustic response (with a small electrical input, otherwise you blow out your speakers). Another way to say this is that the greater the efficiency of a speaker, the less power is needed from an amplifier.

When you design a sound system for your backyard, you need to think about how much space it will serve, how it may impact your neighbors, what type of music you play, and how it will be used (for dance parties or for meditation?). Other considerations include local building codes, the amount of local ambient noise, the size and layout of your yard, and an estimate of how well sound will be dispersed based on the sound-blocking or sound-enhancing features your yard may have. (For instance, water carries sound and amplifies it, whereas berms of earth or hills will block or absorb sound.)

The easiest way to permanently install an outdoor sound system is to power outdoor

speakers through the multizone receiver that is already connected to your indoor sound system or home theater. You'll need to make sure that you have enough amplifier power to get high-quality sound outdoors, especially in relation to the efficiency of the outdoor speakers you choose.

Run the lines for your sound system as you run them for lighting, in separate PVC pipe conduits (you don't want to risk crossing wires).

Outdoor speaker design

Outdoor speakers come in a limited array of designs:

- *Boxes on brackets:* These are meant to be attached to the exterior walls of your house or in or around your outdoor kitchen, set under the eaves, if possible, for weather protection and for bass enhancement. You can run the wiring through the walls of your building or surface-mount them with weather protection. The higher you mount the speakers on the building, the greater the sound projection will be, so if distant sound is one of your goals, this is the way to go. However, if mounted too high you won't be able to hear well when you are close to or under the speakers, so it's a delicate balance. All in all, this design is the one most experts recommend. Look for speakers with stainless steel brackets (for a long, rust-free life) and hardy exteriors. The speakers must be designed specifically for outdoor use.

- A variation on this design are *box columns,* which are tall, thin speakers meant to be placed on decks or patios much like box speakers in a living room. You can run their wires under a deck or along the ground before you build a patio.

- *Multidirectional speakers* are like posts with music—the sound emerges from all sides of a circular speaker at the top, making sound travel in all directions. These speakers are designed to be planted in the middle of an area to send the sound around the yard. Their wires must be buried below ground, preferably in a protective conduit.

- *Faux rock speakers:* Many faux rocks are multidirectional; some high-end models take this into account and have built in upward-facing sound. Faux rocks require buried wire both to look realistic and to protect the wire. Although they are made to blend invisibly into the landscape, one source suggested, with some sarcasm, that multidirectional faux rocks be hung in trees to create the best sound, because situating sound at ground level is really only best for speakers located next to hot tubs or blankets on the grass. Makers of more expensive upward-facing sound systems encased in faux rocks say that their versions can create great sound when thoughtfully located.

Planting Your Outdoor Kitchen

Plants can be agents of magic—they soften up hard areas, making transitions between a built area like a patio and the lawn. They protect you from wind and sun, offering dappled shade and tempering breezes by their very presence. Plants can give you privacy, creating intimate nooks invisible to passersby, as well as function like screens to hide eyesores. Plants can also act architecturally, defining boundaries and offering focal points. White-flowering plants glow at dusk, creating an evening garden, whereas night-blooming flowers offer visual pleasures and haunting fragrances. In the landscape around an outdoor kitchen, plants can further offer gifts for the table in the form of herbs or fruits or vegetables.

Use of trees and shrubs

You can plant trees or shrubs to mark the edges of an outdoor room, either by placing one at each corner or by making a circle of

Dense plantings provide privacy in this garden, where the dining area is tucked into a corner of the terrace. The pergola shades and screens activity from the house above, and its support trellis offers side-to-side privacy between one part of the garden and another.

ABOVE: This path of irregular flagstones is interplanted with creeping herbs. Plantings edging the path soften the geometry of the walkway.

FACING PAGE: Verdant plantings follow the contours of the stonework to fill this dining area with color. Near to the ground, growing plants spill on the patio, as massed plantings gradually step up in scale to the tallest plants that form the back edge of the border. Massing several plants of one variety together makes each area of color and form distinct.

and wide they will ultimately be, so that you won't have to prune excessively. In short, pick your plant materials wisely—you may be living with them for many years to come.

Planting paths

Imagine a wide expanse of green lawn stretching from the back door to the barbecue area at the far end. Now imagine the same lawn bisected evenly with a straight path between house and grill that's fringed with flowers on both sides. Or think of the

trees around a central area. Dwarf weeping crab-apple trees planted in the four corners of a square would create a dramatic and intimate room, whereas a single mature umbrella-shaped tree like a Camperdown elm or weeping willow can create a whole shady "room" underneath its great pendulous branches, suitable for a table and chairs or a picnic on the ground. In contrast, tall, thin cypresses could mark four corners with elegant brevity. High, leafy trees planted at regular intervals can form the "walls" of a room, particularly when their branches are pruned 6 ft. to 8 ft. up their trunks, creating the effect of a high ceiling. Big pots of bamboo (which is often invasive when planted directly in the ground) can be used to form corners or borders of outdoor rooms, as can potted trees.

If you intend to plant a hedge for privacy, research it carefully, because you'll need to select trees or shrubs that grow in a form that will create a dense wall of green. Also find out how fast your proposed plants actually grow (otherwise you may be waiting for years to have your hedge) and how tall

Our Method for Weeding a Brick Patio and Gravel Walk

Weeds have an amazing ability to thrive in even the most inhospitable places. Our antique brick patios and gravel walkways nourish a wide variety of interlopers. We've tried planting creeping thyme between the bricks to crowd out weeds, but it doesn't grow well enough to make a difference. We also poured boiling water over the cracks, sprayed with various weed killers (including vinegar), and weeded by hand. Some years ago we bought a flame thrower (sometimes called a torch-weeder). Configured a bit like a vacuum cleaner, this device has a long hose with a burner at one end and an LP cylinder at the other. (A blow torch could be used, but it is much smaller, it would take much longer, and it would keep you bent over for hours.) Now we burn the weeds in the cracks between the bricks of the patio once a month in summer. We use scraps of cement board propped in front of the edging plants to protect them, then aim the flame at each section of the patio in turn until all the weeds and seeds are incinerated. We do the same thing along the weedy surface of the gravel walk. It's brutal and exhilarating in equal measure, and the clean, weed-free patio is ample reward.

Container Planting 101

When choosing plants for a container, you can take two routes—massed or mixed planting. Both can create tremendous visual impact—think of a big pot filled to exploding with bright red salvia or a composition of purple heliotrope, white geraniums, and pink and white striped petunias spilling down the side. If you're going to go with a single plant, make sure it's one with a long blooming season, unless you don't mind replanting every four weeks or so. If mixed plantings appeal, again, be mindful of time and length of bloom, because if you plant them together, you'll want them to bloom together. For interesting composition, mix short and tall, specimen and filler plants, and contrast textures and colors. For example, have some trailing plants along the front edges and gradually build height toward the center of the pot. Consider, too, if you're arranging a collection of container plants together in different pots, how to create vertical accents as punctuation to a series of lower plants.

Set on a stone pedestal that matches it in color, this stone and resin pot is filled with annuals that spill over the sides. This planter works well because the flowers are all the same scale, and their pink and white blossoms are a pleasing contrast to their green foliage.

path curving sensuously around thickly planted oval beds of flowers. You can see from this exercise that paths (and their shape and ornamentation) have enormous visual impact.

The planting that edges a path can be a real opportunity to enhance the landscape of your property. In an area with little rainfall, use drought-tolerant plants with scent and bloom, such as one of the many flowering salvias (sage). In areas with lots of rain, plant a classic mixed herbaceous perennial border. Coastal gardeners may want to edge their paths with hardy rugosa roses, whereas those in very Mediterranean climates may choose lavender or rosemary. Alternatively, you can copy Monet's garden and set your paths under hoop arches at regular intervals, each planted with vines to make a long, leafy tunnel, edged at ground level with trailing nasturtiums. Whatever

you choose, you'll want to make the plantings close to a path as fragrant and attractive as you can, so they enhance the experience of moving from place to place.

Bear in mind that you can also interplant the actual walkway surface with creeping herbs such as thyme for even more fragrance and sensual delight. Such plants can go between pavers of landscape stone or concrete, bricks, or other elements, or can edge the innermost sides of a pathway.

Edging around a patio
A patio is frequently the site of an outdoor kitchen or outdoor entertaining area. It doesn't look its best, though, if it's an island of equipment or furniture floating in an open expanse—it needs plants to frame the action and make a transition between the hard materials of the patio and the softer grass around it.

The purpose of planting edging around a patio is twofold: to soften the edges of the built surface and to integrate the patio into the landscape. Edge plantings should look a little wild, thick, and blowsy, because this makes for a more natural-looking transition. Of course, when plants are young and newly planted, they rarely look thick and wild. You can make this less obvious by either buying more mature, larger specimens or using quick-growing annuals interplanted with slower-growing perennials

to make the first growing season lush with bloom. Also, set the plants closer together than is normally recommended to produce a more abundant look; you can either divide or reposition them later on when they start crowding each other. You can also fill containers with closely planted annuals or bulbs and set them in the planted beds to fill in and provide added height and interest. In choosing plants, look for some that can trail and spill onto the patio and balance those with plants that offer vertical accents and interesting leaf shapes, colors, and textures.

You can also create raised beds around a patio, either in wooden boxes or by hilling up the earth and setting stone or concrete edgers to keep the dirt in place. Raised beds bring the plants closer to you and make it easier to weed, because you don't have to bend down as far.

As you select the plants to border your patio, include some that offer intoxicating scent when the sun goes down. They give a garden a whole other dimension of delight.

Container planting

Container plantings offer a number of virtues—in box form, they break up long horizontal spaces, whether at floor level on patios, decks, or porches, or along railings. Rectangular planting boxes made for floor

Wisteria Watch

Wisteria, a plant known for its gorgeous, fragrant bloom, is available in many hybrid forms, but it has its problems: It can be fussy as to soil and it can refuse to flower for its first ten or fifteen years (or it can bloom after two to three years). Most problematic of all, it is so strong that, once it gets going, it can tear down almost any support. When wisteria is allowed to soar through tall trees in the South, it eventually kills them by strangulation. If you decide to grow wisteria up the side of a gazebo or to cover a pergola, train it carefully, securing it to the structure but not allowing it to wrap around a support, weave itself between supports, or insinuate itself up under shingles and siding. Prune it regularly, both for flower production and shape. Such vigilance can be well rewarded by each year's absolutely astonishing floral display.

level can function as privacy screens when planted with dense, tall plants such as bamboo. They can also define the boundaries of a dining area, or direct traffic to the outdoor kitchen or to the front or back door. Use planting boxes or regular flower pots to grow food crops in small spaces, making the outdoor kitchen a place to harvest as well as prepare food.

Railing boxes are designed to sit astride porch or deck railings with a notch in the underside to accommodate a rail or with hardware to attach the planter to the inside or outside edge of a railing. They act like window boxes, bringing blossom and scent to the level of a sitting person's head and offering a chance to garden without bending. If your grill is set on a deck, plant railing boxes with herbs and edible flowers so you can pluck flavor elements as you cook.

Other planting options include wall-mounted planting baskets that can be attached to posts as well as to brackets mounted on walls to create vertical interest. In addition, you can furnish your outdoor area with tall plants or small trees in pots to create vertical accents.

THE SCALE OF CONTAINERS

When choosing a container, think about the best size for the location—a row of puny pots will look silly edging a deck, but could look wonderful in niches ranged along the wall of an outdoor stairway, where their intimate scale will work. For edging a large expanse of a dining or entertaining deck or patio, only pots of good size will provide a clear boundary and hold plants big enough to make a statement against the landscape in the distance. When arranging a series of pots, whether large or small, punch up the overall impact by repeating the same flowers in every pot.

Raising the bottom of your container off the surface of a wooden deck or porch keeps the wood from discoloring due to damp, as well as aids in bringing much-needed air circulation to the roots of the plant. Plastic saucers will protect the deck, whereas using pot feet or placing shards of broken tile or small rocks in the saucer will lift up the pot for air.

Planting retaining walls

Retaining walls of any height offer a wonderful environment for planting—the tops are perfect for alpine plants, and cascading plants can spill over the top onto the wall. There are both upright and creeping forms of many culinary herbs, a nice addition to retaining walls built near the outdoor kitchen.

Retaining walls can be planted on their outward-facing side if they are built from stone without mortar. Planting pockets are created by filling spaces with soil and small plants as you go along; tiny plants can also be placed later, held in position by moss until they take hold. Some plants can be seeded directly into soil-filled wall pockets.

The area in front of a retaining wall is also prime garden real estate, as plants look wonderful against stone. Starting from the wall, plant tall plants first, then medium height plants, then small upright plants, and finally spillers to trail and soften the front boundary of your flower bed.

Trellis or column planting

Training plants up columns or posts can provide vertical accents in an open setting, as well as disguise difficult places such as the area beneath a deck. The base of the deck and the actual underdeck area are almost always a problem, in part because the amount of sun they receive is usually extremely limited. If you are lucky enough to have the base of the deck area in some light, you can put up lattice or other screening material or secure eye hooks at deck and ground level and run wire or garden string between them. Then allow annual or perennial vines, or vertical food crops like squash or grapes, to grow up them (if you're using string, though, lighter-weight annual vines like morning glories are a better choice).

Around a patio, vines of all kinds can be trained up posts or columns, covering them with leafy accents and/or blooms. You could even string horizontal chains between columns and prune and train long-caned roses along them. If you are feeling ambitious, espalier fruit trees such as apples along horizontal wires attached to regular posts planted next to the trunks of the trees, creating a living wall. Finally, vines can be trained up hoops, posts,

Vines to Climb Your Outdoor Kitchen

Some vines twine through interstices, some cling by pads, others attach by way of tendrils: Make sure to match your vine to its means of support. Ordinary ivy *(Hedera)* can make a great wall of green on the side of a house or along a fence. Parthenocissus, which looks much like ivy, turns a glorious shade of red in fall. Trumpet vine *(Campsis radicans)* grows so vigorously that it may need restraining, but its bright flowers and shading leaves make it a welcome old-fashioned choice. Several kinds of honeysuckle mature into excellent fence covers. Sweet pea pulls itself up via tendrils for a colorful annual screen and is wonderfully fragrant. Both annual and perennial hops can be trained on fences and poles. Clematis puts on an impressive display in spring or summer (depending on the species), trained up posts or across trellising. Autumn clematis *(Clematis paniculata)* is a particularly enthusiastic grower and will reward you with a sweetly scented cloud of small white flowers that can cover an arbor in its entirety. Climbing long-caned roses can be tied to trellises on the side of a building or arbor or draped profusely along a fence. Mandevilla, a tender vine that can be overwintered inside, is an avid climber, twining around columns or guy wires and covering itself with large, fragrant, showy pink or white flowers.

Striped clematis 'Nelly Moser' offers a spectacular show when in bloom, and forms a lush screen in season.

topiary forms, or columns to grow over a trellis or pergola to create a living ceiling.

PLANTING A PERGOLA

Although pergolas are beautiful in their own right, they come to life, literally, when covered with growing plants. Whether you choose to plant climbing roses, wisteria, grapes, or other vines, your pergola will be transformed into an unforgettable outdoor room. Take care, however, because the plants you choose need to be matched to the location of the structure, as well as its sturdiness and proximity to the house.

Grapes are a traditional choice for a pergola, and training grapevines up the posts and then up and over the roof is a beautiful way to have a living "room." To do this, you must have a sunny, well-drained location and need to choose grapes that are suitable for your climate. Because grapes are vigorous growers, they need very little encouragement to make their way up a pole or ladder, requiring only the odd tie to keep them on the path of your choosing.

Fragrance in the Night Kitchen

It's such a great experience to sit outside in the evening, surrounded by aromatic flowers, that it's worth the effort to create a dedicated night-blooming and/or fragrant garden near your outdoor kitchen or dining area. The following is a list of night-blooming annuals with haunting fragrances:

Evening stock (*Matthiola longipetala*)
Flowering tobacco (*Nicotiana*)
Four o'clock (*Mirabilis jalapa*)
Jimson weed (*Datura*)
Moonflower (*Ipomoea alba*)
Night-flowering catchfly (*Silene noctiflora*)
Sun drops (*Oenothera*)

There are a number of wonderfully fragrant perennials, vines, and shrubs too, although they are not necessarily more strongly scented at night. These include the following:

Confederate jasmine (*Trachelospermum jasminoides*)
Daphne (*Daphne odora*)
Evening primrose (*Oenothera Biennis*)
Gas plant (*Dictamnus albus*)
Heliotrope (*Heliotropium*)
Honeysuckle (*Lonicera*)
Indian carnation (*Tabernaemontana divaricate 'Flore Pelno'*)
Lilac (*Syringa*)
Lily (*Lilium*)
Mock orange (*Philadelphus*)
Night phlox, such as 'Midnight Candy'
Night-blooming cereus (*Epiphyllum oxypetalum*)
Night-blooming jessamine (*Cestrum nocturnum*)
Rose
Sweet almond verbena (*Aloysia virgata*)
Sweet rocket (*Hesperis*)
Wisteria

LEFT: Long-caned roses have been trained and tied to grow up and around the posts of this pergola. The elements in this pergola repeat and mirror to create overall harmony: The pink roses on one side and white roses on the other are all of the same scale, and they twine up identical white posts, marching in a row. It would be quite different if the roses were of many different colors.

FACING PAGE: Even urban settings can support decorative and food crops—here, the rafters of the pergola support gourds that hang over the dining area.

FACING PAGE: It is possible to make a stream that looks as natural as this one, provided you choose your site well. Dig your trench, line it with rubber, edge it with stones and aquatic plants, use appropriate plants, and provide electric aeration.

LEFT: Water features such as this fountain provide a variety of pleasures: They offer the music of dripping water, can humidify nearby plantings, and are beautiful in their own right.

Adding Water to Your Outdoor Room

Water features, whether large or small, add another dimension to a yard or garden, because they offer tranquil sound and a sense of coolness (this is particularly true of fountains). These days, you can't find a garden center that doesn't sell pond liners, ready-made freeform pond shells, and other water-feature containers, pumps, fountains, and aquatic plants—what was once exotic and hard to find has become easy to locate and install.

Some water features are designed for small situations, such as wall-hung fountains or waterfalls, which can even be used on a balcony. Lightweight, often made of fiberglass, and colored to look antique, they have tiny pumps that have to be plugged in. A compact water feature can be placed almost anywhere, depending on its size. A fountain near the outdoor kitchen offers the soothing sound of running water, which is equally welcome near the dining area. Keep in mind that some fountains may spray and create a fine mist that can soak into decks and cause mold. Often you can adjust the strength of the spray, but if that's not possible, you may want to play it safe by locating a fountain on or over a bed of gravel (for drainage) and/or put moisture-loving plants below and in front of the fountain to catch and benefit from the humidity.

Ponds, which are constructed using either preformed pools or from lengths of pond liner, sit on an excavated and shaped bed of sand and/or felt or landscape cloth to protect the liner from sharp roots. The pond liner is held in place by water. Rocks, small stones, and gravel are added along the edge to hide the pond liner and create a more natural look. A submersible pump is set in the water to keep it moving and discourage algae and mosquito larvae. After the water has settled for a period of days or weeks (depending on the pond size), plants and even fish can be introduced. Ponds look most natural when set at the lowest point in the landscape, at the place where they naturally would form from the drainage of higher land around them.

Such a water feature can create a focal point or view from the deck or patio, and should be carefully located with that in mind. Avoid placing water features close to trees that shed their leaves, plant the edges with appropriate plants (shade lovers for shade, sun lovers for a bright location), and consider aquatic plants and fish to add even more life to the water.

Small ponds need aerators and filters as well as pumps. If you are planning an ambitious pond with a fountain, you may want to light the fountain from below to create a beautiful evening vista to enjoy from your outdoor space. Be sure to plan outlets for any electric-powered water features you may want now or in the future. Such outlets need to be grounded and approved for outdoor use, and should be positioned to be as unobtrusive as possible. For large water features such as ponds, it's useful to have a hose outlet nearby. (Small water features such as wall fountains use recirculating water and can be filled with a watering can.)

In Conclusion

We have now covered all the steps in conceiving and building an outdoor kitchen, including choosing a site, planning your outdoor kitchen's geography, considering every cooking and noncooking option, designing dining and entertaining areas, planting and furnishing outdoor spaces, and thinking about sound and lighting.

Given the range of choices and amenities at every price point and in so many styles, I hope you'll feel that it's easy to create a great outdoor kitchen that perfectly suits the way you live. No matter what you choose, you can make fabulous food and experience the full range of sensual delights that enhance an outdoor room, from light effects, music, and flickering fire, to water features and beautiful places to plant herbs and flowers, to the comfort of heat on a chilly night.

Enjoy!

A Vermont Hillside Transformed

When I decided to write this book, I also decided to build an outdoor kitchen as a way to fully research the topic, to create a case study of the design process, and to explore firsthand many of the issues that come up when building an outdoor kitchen. This is the first time I've built something at the same time I've written about it, and it has been instructive. It has helped to remind me how stressful building decisions (and their accompanying

ABOVE: When the nights turn chill, this powerful patio heater almost makes you believe that autumn will never come.

LEFT: Looking through a cedar arbor, the original freestanding outdoor kitchen is on the left. The two round patios are made of antique brick and meet the curve of the brick front walk.

From the small front deck located right off the indoor kitchen, the freestanding grills are hardly visible in a half-hidden alcove shielded by a dwarf crab-apple tree and other plantings

financial decisions) are, and it was a welcome opportunity to illustrate many of the design points I make in this book, as well to detail the process of making those decisions.

Where I Started

We live in a renovated 200-year-old post-and-beam hay barn converted into a home; my husband and I have been working on it for more than two decades. Although most of our attention has gone into the interior of the house, we've also had a wonderful front garden for the last 12 years, designed by Dutch landscape designer Edwin de Bruijn.

For as long as we've had the front entrance garden it has held our portable outdoor kitchen set on the far side of our south-facing patios, hidden in an alcove created by a dwarf weeping crab-apple tree. That kitchen consisted of a gas grill, a charcoal grill, and a worktable—the quintessential simple outdoor kitchen. Near it, in the center of the adjoining area, an umbrella-topped table and chairs created a sheltered dining area. The patios, two "kissing" circles made of antique bricks, are surrounded by mixed herbaceous perennials and more than forty antique and hardy roses. A hidden fountain on the bank beyond the table bubbles through a pierced stone set over a buried basin, providing water music. From the patios on one side, a curving brick walk leads to the front door, past the front deck and through a cedar arbor flanked by climbing roses and wisteria. On the far side of the patios are a lawn and stone walls, with two terraces planted with more roses and other perennials. A third path leads around the far side of the building to the backyard.

Facing the front walk and overlooking the brick circles, our small wooden front deck has always been a cherished spot for morning coffee. It offers full sun early in the day and a view of the gardens just steps from the kitchen.

Although we were quite happy with our simple kitchen for many years, the opportunity to create a more permanent and expanded outdoor kitchen was exciting. Ever since we discovered that our indoor masonry oven made the house too hot to use it

during the summer, we'd fantasized about having an outdoor masonry oven as well. We also had become more ambitious in our cooking over time, and wanted to further explore smoking, smoke-grilling, and other more outdoor cooking methods. We also wanted to be able to grill and barbecue outdoors in the winter, and that was hard to do with portable equipment kept under wraps in cold and snowy weather. As a result, our initial requirements were a place for a permanent masonry oven, a roof overhead that would shed snow, and a location not too far from the house.

Choosing a New Outdoor Location

For me, the most useful lesson in choosing a building site has been to first consider those

Looking toward the back of the house from the north field, the screen porch is at left and the freestanding kitchen pavilion is on the far right. The two-level deck is supported by columns; some portions of the underdeck are capped by arches, whereas others are faced with custom lattice and cutouts. The ramp that connects the second story to the outside is on the right, with the underramp passage beneath it that connects the front garden to the rear. In the foreground, stone terraces have been thickly planted with a perennial wildflower mix to make a colorful show come next summer.

areas of your property in greatest need of beautification. Because our front garden was already lovely, it was painful to imagine tearing it up to make a more permanent kitchen there. Yet there were still reasons to consider it as a site: It's very close to the indoor kitchen and would have offered great convenience, particularly in winter. It would also have eliminated the need for an outdoor sink, refrigerator, or storage—convincing arguments from both a space and a financial perspective.

The drawbacks of this location were also compelling: We'd have to look at the kitchen all the time through the front windows, smoke would rise to the bedroom windows above, it would involve destroying part of a garden we had worked hard to establish, and, because it would be next to the front walk, every visitor to the house would see every detail of it as they walked to the front door, making it seem like a trophy kitchen.

Behind the house on the north side we had a rotting wooden back deck that needed replacing and a steeply sloping back yard that was virtually untouched, aside from some terraced gardens. Above those terraces and obscuring the view of the western meadow was a neglected area filled with weeds, brush, and saplings.

Our Decision

After much debate, we decided to locate the outdoor kitchen in back on the north and west sides of the house. Although significantly farther away from the indoor kitchen, it offered greater privacy and allowed us to concentrate our efforts on an area in need of attention. It also meant that we could rebuild the deck and have a small screened porch near the indoor living room and kitchen, so we could take advantage of the long views from the cool, shady north

side of the building during the summer, with its sunset vistas to the west above the meadow. There was, however, a price for this choice—we had to pay for earthmoving and leveling, as well as for landscaping and installing hardscape.

Each area of these proposed outdoor rooms needed even more careful thought, in part because we had to articulate what was wrong with the area in order to figure out how we wanted it to change. For example, our deck had never worked. At 50 ft. long and 12 ft. off the ground, it had two problems. First, it was distanced from the landscape by virtue of its height. We wanted the new deck to connect us to the landscape, not separate us. Second, because it was so long (paralleling the length of the house), it felt like being on the deck of a ship far above the ocean, and it was difficult to create specific areas for conversation, for cooking, and for eating that felt natural. The new deck needed areas with clear boundaries and functions.

Once we began to imagine the deck, we could see how to relate it to a little kitchen pavilion just beyond where the deck would end, near the side passage from the front of the house on the west side of the building. Because the outdoor kitchen was going to be some distance from the indoor kitchen, we knew we wanted to add running water. Fortunately, because the location is close to the corner of the building, it was relatively easy to extend electrical connections and drainable water lines to the site.

Using an Architect to Achieve Our Goals

We hired renovation architect Andy Armstrong to design the built areas of the project. Even though Andy lives and works in Atlanta, he was able to do much of the

design work long distance based on measurements and photographs we provided him, supplemented by lots of conversations. We had an initial meeting in Atlanta, and Andy sketched designs as we talked. All of his finished plans were based on ideas we discussed at our initial four-hour consultation.

We went into the consultation with lots of measurements, photographs, and a list of things we wanted. We knew we wanted an outdoor kitchen pavilion with a hipped roof as close to the end of the deck as possible. We had a long list of equipment desires, including a powerful gas grill for fast everyday cooking, along with side burners so we could prepare whole meals, whether breakfast, lunch, or dinner, completely outdoors with ease. We chose a model that offered a number of options for the side burners:

a wok burner and a griddle, as well as two regular gas burners. For great grill smoking and charcoal flavor, we wanted to include the Big Green Egg in the finished kitchen. And because we had a desire for real slow-cooked barbecue without paying it endless attention, we wanted a reliable small under-counter electric smoker. Finally, for summer high-heat roasting and pizza under the stars, we dreamed of a big masonry oven that could feed a crowd. In addition, so we wouldn't have to trek back and forth from the indoor kitchen, we wanted space for an outdoor undercounter refrigerator as well as storage for dishware and equipment.

We also knew we wanted the deck off the house to have at least two levels, establishing a relationship with the landscape, and with distinct areas for different kinds of activities, such as dining and lounging and

Inside the screened porch, deep outdoor soft seating adds great comfort. The sky blue upholstery is similar in color to the couches in the interior living room, just inside the house on the other side of this wall. Because the porch is visible all year around from the interior windows, it made sense to keep the colors compatible.

On the lower deck, two chaise longues are angled to catch sunsets above the meadow. Long steps add lots of seating when there's a crowd, and subtle step lights and post lights provide illumination. The dining area is just beyond, on the upper deck, between the screened porch and lower deck. Three large fiberglass planters provide blossoms in summer and can withstand winter weather.

parties. We wanted the deck to be made of composite decking, a green and durable material strong enough to withstand snow falling off the roof of the house. We wanted the supporting structure of the deck and outdoor kitchen to be as durable as possible (in the end we specified Wolmanized® lumber, a kind of pressure treatment that uses copper as a preservative, for both the underdeck and the posts and beams of the outdoor kitchen).

Finally, our wish list included a screened porch to use as an outdoor living room that would block as little light as possible to the living room indoors.

The Result

Andy delivered designs for all of what we wanted and more—he embellished the underdeck with arches and custom lattice, turning what is usually a problem area into an asset; he designed the lower deck to cre-

ate angles that encourage intimacy and conversation; and he added all possible charm to the outdoor kitchen pavilion.

The upper deck connects to the attic storage of the garage/barn on one end, and ground level at the other side. Andy specified a 12-ft. by 14-ft. screened porch at the barn end, off the indoor living room, to create an intimate outdoor living room. The 4-ft.-square venting skylight with a remote control provides both light and fresh air; the skylight also brings more natural light into the house through the corresponding window. Perhaps best of all, it has a rain sensor, which closes the skylight in inclement weather. On the deck next to the screened porch is an open-air dining area, right in front of the French doors to the interior living room, convenient both to the indoor kitchen and the new outdoor kitchen. The rest of the deck descends one level to form an open sitting area, bounded

Looking back at the outdoor kitchen pavilion from the tip of the patio, the house is in the background and the high mountain meadow is to the right. The pavers are pigmented concrete, inset with bluestone to form a dining area rug. Landscape fixtures aim light down to minimize light pollution and to increase safety after dark. Uplights, downlights, and an atmospheric light inside the cupola make the outdoor kitchen useful at any hour.

The dining end of the kitchen patio offers the best view of the western meadow. Bluestone stepping-stones invite guests to walk on the grass.

dates six people. Down a few steps on the deck, two linen-cushioned chaise longues offer prime seating for views of the meadow and sunset. (We positioned the outdoor speakers under the eaves of the building, so they sound their best on the deck.) On the outdoor kitchen patio, bar-stool seating and a matching four-person umbrella table and chairs offer convenient places for dining and socializing.

Across the path from the end of the deck where it meets the ground is the outdoor kitchen pavilion, a small, hip-roofed pavilion. In order to house all the equipment we wanted, it has a little back extension to accommodate the bulk of the wood-fired pizza oven. A cedar shake roof with a louvered copper-roofed cupola creates shelter and provides a chimney effect for smoke and grease, aided by a powerful ceiling fan.

Getting the Project Built

We hired a contractor and his crew to build the project for a contract price that included construction, electric, plumbing, and roofing. The project was originally scheduled for completion in five weeks, but ended up stretching intermittently over five months. Although this delay did not increase the cost of the project, it certainly increased our stress level. One little-considered aspect of renovation or construction is the difficulty of losing one's privacy. Having a carpentry crew in residence off and on for many months is not easy, even when they are mostly working outside.

Using a Landscape Designer

Unfortunately, scars left by the contractor's inexperienced excavator when leveling the site for the kitchen pavilion made it necessary to do much more extensive landscaping than we had anticipated. It was at this

by long steps that can serve as additional seating.

We furnished the screen porch with comfortable soft seating. The powder-coated aluminum furniture used everywhere in the project was available in a wide choice of colors and finishes, and we coordinated the screen porch furniture colors with those of the adjoining living room, visible through the porch window. On the deck, a long dining table with an umbrella and comfortable sling chairs is convenient and accommo-

point that we asked landscape architect Edwin de Bruijn to return. He rose to the challenge by creating a masterful plan that included a diagonal patio that matched Andy's diagonal deck, with soft plantings around the borders set with large sitting stones. He designed, planted, and built all of the rustic stone steps that provide access to the outdoor kitchen patio, as well as those that go down to the stone wall terraces. In creating his plan, he seamlessly integrated the outdoor kitchen with all of the new construction. He also created a new dining patio near the outdoor kitchen that takes advantage of the best view on the property: the long vistas of a mountain meadow.

This unanticipated landscaping and hardscaping expense added about 30 percent to the total cost of the project, but also greatly increased the beauty of the finished area.

Lighting the Project

As the scale of the project grew, with the addition of the patio off the outdoor kitchen plus the paths and stone steps down to the

Two outer sides of the kitchen pavilion have a dining bar with armchair stool-height seating. The projection on the left side of the building is the masonry oven, encased in white stucco and roofed in metal. The undercounter electric smoker is just visible straight ahead inside the kitchen pavilion.

The hot zone: In the outdoor kitchen, the hot zone is made up of the undercounter electric smoker, the big gas grill and two side burners, the charcoal-fueled Big Green Egg, and the large masonry oven. Because the oven is a monolithic floor-to-ceiling presence, I centered it on the back wall, with only its face actually in the outdoor kitchen pavilion (it has its own little roof and chimney, and is covered in stucco). On the run of counter around the corner to the right of the oven, I located the rest of the hot zone

ABOVE: Fixtures facing upward illuminate the roof structure and provide ambient light, whereas those angled down toward the counters supply task lighting. The cupola light makes it glow from the outside through the louvers. Carpentry details like shaped rafter tails add interest, as do the subtly shaped angle braces on the post-and-beam frame.

RIGHT: Stepping-stones connect the stone steps down to the wildflower terraces with the stone path between the deck and outdoor kitchen. Hooded lights mark the path at dusk.

terraces, it became clear that the lighting requirements were more complex than we had anticipated. We turned to Vista Professional Outdoor Lighting for help, and they sent us their regional representative, Thom Petrush, who came and created a light plan for the whole project. This included landscape lighting for the patio, paths, and steps, as well as post and step lighting for the deck and extraordinary ambient and task lighting for the outdoor kitchen. Similar advice can be had from dedicated outdoor-lighting retailers around the country.

The Outdoor Kitchen in Detail

In laying out the kitchen I used the four-zone principle I created and always use when thinking about kitchen design. Each zone stands alone, and each zone has counter areas between appliances.

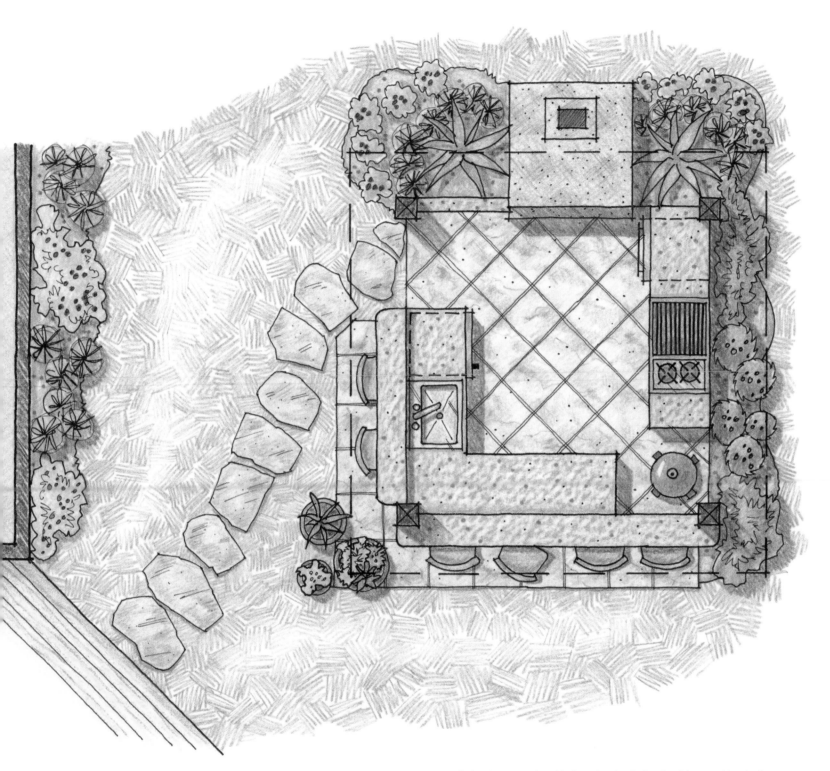

The kitchen is divided into zones for storage and use. As fitting for an outdoor kitchen that is all about outdoor cooking techniques, the Hot zone takes up two legs of the kitchen—the back wall, which holds the wood-fired oven, and the adjacent leg, which holds the electric smoker, gas grill and side burners, and the Big Green Egg. The Dry zone is the only area without any cooking equipment—it holds storage for plates and utencils, and has pull-out double garbage bins in the cabinets, along with numerous drawers. The Dry zone counter holds the food processor, blender, knives and cutting boards, and functions as the primary food prep zone. The next leg holds the sink (Wet zone) and the under-counter refridgerator (Cold zone).

A great deal of working kitchen can be fit in a 10-ft. square. Wood for the masonry oven is stored in a cavity below the hearth; near it is a pot holding tall pizza tools. At left, shallow shelves hold stemware and glasses. The hot zone counter at right holds all the other cooking equipment: an undercounter electric smoker, a gas grill with two side burners, and the charcoal-fueled Big Green Egg. An undercounter refrigerator is just beyond the sink, at left, next to the doorway into the pavilion. Above, the galvanized fan moves smoke and grease up and out the cupola.

appliances—the smoker and both grills—with runs of counter in between.

The dry zone: Turning the next corner, I made that whole side of the room into the dry zone, a dedicated food preparation area without any appliances. It faces the dining patio and one of the sitting bars, allowing the cook to chat with guests.

The wet and cold zones: To the right, I made the last wall of the kitchen into the wet and cold zones, which consist of a big soapstone apron-front sink and, to its right, an undercounter refrigerator. Because I made the kitchen around four sides of a small (10 ft.) square, it's essentially a one-, two-, or three-person kitchen. But

ABOVE: Corn caramelizes on the grill while bacon cooks on the side-burner griddle. Having a side burner with optional attachments offers lots of versatility: This model also includes a wok burner and two regular gas burners.

RIGHT: Cooking in a wood-burning oven is not limited to pizza. Here, stuffed, rolled, and tied boneless leg of lamb and local potatoes roast together in a cast iron frying pan. To the left and middle of the oven, a tall earthenware casserole holds white beans, garlic, and sage that cook at the same time.

because it is ringed by eating bars and bar seating, it can accommodate lots of guests at once.

The materials

Because I wanted the kitchen counter to be durable and weatherproof, I specified Vermont soapstone for the countertops, eating bars, and sink. The backsplash tiles are also soapstone, laid closely together without grout. Above the sink, I chose an articulated wall-mounted faucet that could reach every part of the big sink, but fold back when not in use.

The cabinets are stainless steel outdoor models fitted with drawers (except for the sink and grill cabinets, which have doors). In the drawers, there's space for cooking tools, flatware, dishes, mixing bowls, and table linen. Shallow wooden shelves built in near the entrance to the pavilion on one side of the masonry oven hold stemware and glasses. In the dry zone there is also an undercounter pull-out trash cabinet, which holds two bins for garbage and recycling. The undersink cabinet holds a compost bucket, biodegradable dish soap, and cleaning supplies. The sink drains directly into the garden.

The floor is made of the same pigmented Belgard® concrete pavers as the rest of the patio, laid on a foundation of sand and crushed stone, and installed at a very slight grade for drainage. The field above the kitchen and patio has a swale cut into it, to direct water away from the kitchen area. The entire patio is ringed with flowers and flowering shrubs, and the area closest to the kitchen is planted with a variety of culinary herbs, set amidst a stone rip-rap retaining wall.

How It Could Have Been Done in Stages

ad we not been on a deadline to finish the whole project for this book, we could have built it in stages.

Stage 1: Designing and Planning
To build a complex project over time, it is crucial to have a good architectural plan, a landscape plan, and a map for utilities, as well as any necessary permits. Commissioning such plans would be a logical first stage.

Stage 2: Building the Deck and Screen Porch
The second stage would have been to build, light, and furnish the new deck and screen porch, and to relocate the portable cooking equipment onto the end of the deck near the outdoor kitchen site. This would have given us an opportunity to audition the spot for a whole summer, assessing the location, the lighting, and the views.

In addition, the outdoor sound system could have been installed, with speakers mounted high on the building, just under the roof. Containers filled with plants could be set along the deck, and landscaping could proceed around the underdeck area. Additional equipment such as a patio heater and/or propane-fueled mosquito-control unit could also have been purchased.

Stage 3: Preparing the Land and Utilities, Building the Masonry Oven
The third stage would have been to clear and level the land where the permanent outdoor kitchen was to be, lay out and bury the water and electric lines, dig and pour the footings for the pavilion posts, and pour the masonry oven pad. The permanent masonry oven could be installed at this point, because it's a stand-alone with its own roof. The portable equipment would remain on the end of the deck, not too far from the permanent oven.

Stage 4: Installing the Patio, Planting the Landscape, Installing Outdoor Lighting, and Moving the Portable Equipment to a New Location
The fourth stage would have been to install the hardscape—particularly the patio pavers—and to begin landscaping around the area with plants. The outdoor lighting could be installed along the paths and around the patio, and the new patio umbrella table and chairs could be placed. The portable cooking equipment could then be placed on the site of the permanent kitchen until the next phase was completed.

Stage 5: Building the Outdoor Kitchen Pavilion, Furnishing and Finishing It
The final stage would be to complete the project—build the outdoor kitchen pavilion and install the outdoor cooking equipment, refrigerator, sink, cabinets, counters, and pavilion interior lighting.

My Favorite Things

In any project, the choices a homeowner makes or a designer specifies are both arbitrary and instructive. That's because there is rarely only one way to do things. However, because outdoor kitchens are subject to all the forces of nature and will have differing requirements due to climate and use, my reasons for choosing particular pieces of equipment or products may be helpful to others confronting similar issues.

- *A 20- in. by 30-in. soapstone apron-front sink:* I love big sinks, and especially when washing vegetables straight from the garden or rinsing big birds for the wood-fired oven, there's nothing like having a sink generous enough for the purpose. Although many people choose small sinks for the outdoors, I was ready to sacrifice counter space to have the largest sink possible.
- *Soapstone counters:* We have the same counters inside the house, and we like their matte surface and quiet, old-fashioned elegance. They are easy to maintain with occasional coatings of mineral oil, and they're great outdoors. We used tiles laid closely as the backsplash, so there are no grout lines.
- *Cedar shingles for the kitchen pavilion:* I wanted the building to have all the diminutive, textured charm of small buildings, and cedar shingles fit the bill.
- *Concrete pavers:* These make a great surface for the kitchen pavilion patio without holding heat in summer, and their color and texture are remarkably natural looking. The same manufacturer makes a special polymeric sand that prevents weeds and ants from overtaking the cobbles, an invaluable addition.
- *Composite wood decking:* We chose a lovely gray color, and it will never need painting and won't rot, split, or warp. It's a green product and attractive to boot. The white vinyl rail system is classic in design, and has a traditional New England appearance.
- *Powder-coated cast aluminum furniture:* I wanted casual furniture that would hold up to family use year after year and still look elegant enough for entertaining. It's incredibly comfortable, extremely well made, and looks like traditional wrought iron. Unlike iron, however, it's not too heavy to move around.
- *High-quality outdoor speakers:* Until building this project, I had no idea what a great pleasure it is to have wonderful sound outdoors using outdoor speakers mounted under the roof overhang.
- *Stainless steel cabinets:* The cabinets for the outdoor kitchen are gorgeous—I like the contrast of matte stone and well-designed shiny steel; I also appreciate how easy it is to sanitize the steel and how weather resistant it is. I particularly appreciate the chance to customize storage by making an all-drawer unit, and I like the pull-out double trash sorter enormously.

Now That It's Done

With the project completed, we can truly say that it has changed our outdoor life. Because the outdoor kitchen is so complete, with sink and refrigerator, stone counters, and cabinet storage, as well as a rich choice of outdoor cooking appliances, it functions perfectly as a kitchen whenever we want to use it. Because we can store all the food we need there, as well as tableware and tools, we don't need to trek from indoor kitchen to outdoor kitchen, and can keep some items outside year round. And even in winter, it's easy to use (except for the sink and refrigerator, which are closed in freezing weather). We can grill or smoke on the coldest of winter days, sheltered under the roof.

FACING PAGE: Using drawers to hold not only flatware and tools but plates, serving bowls, and table linens means that you don't need overhead cabinets. These units are made for outdoor kitchens, and can withstand cold and harsh weather.

LEFT: Looking back toward the deck from the outdoor kitchen pavilion, you can see the relationship between the outdoor rooms and the house. In the foreground, the large apron-front soapstone sink is deep enough to wash lots of fruits and vegetables at one time. The wall-mounted faucet is articulating, and can be folded against the back wall. The undercounter refrigerator is at right.

Resources

Professional Associations

HPBA: Hearth, Patio & Barbecue Association, which represents the manufacturers and retailers of outdoor equipment
www.hpba.org

Casual Furniture Association (furniture and outdoor decorating products)
www.casualfurniture.org

All-in-One Complete Outdoor Kitchen Systems

CalSpas offer a number of complete outdoor kitchens
www.calspas.com

Cook at Home offers a "cabana kitchen" www.cookathomeappliances.com/cabanakitchen/cbk_cabana_kitchen.html

www.outdoorkitchensdepot.com offers an "ultimate outdoor kitchen package deal"

www.vermontislands.com (complete outdoor cooking and entertaining islands)

see also Cabinets

Beer Tap

DCS
www.dcsappliances.com

Summit
www.summitcommercial.com

Marvel
www.marvelindustries.com

Cabinets for the Outdoor Kitchen

Danver
www.danver.com

Werever
www.werever.com

www.kitchenplace.com

www.outdoorkitchenconcepts.com

Casual Furniture

Brown Jordan
www.brownjordan.com

Carter Grandle
www.cartergrandle.com

Lloyd Flanders Outdoor Furniture
(800) 362-2424

Outback Chair Company
www.outbackchair.com

Summer Classics
www.summerclassics.com

Telescope Casual Furniture
www.telescopecasual.com

Tropitone
www.tropitone.com

Charcoal Grills and Smokers

Big Green Egg
www.biggreenegg.com

Charbroil
www.charbroil.com

Char-Griller Grills and Smokers
www.chargriller.com

Hasty Bake
www.hastybake.com

Portable Kitchen Cast Aluminum Cooker
www.pkgrills.com

Weber Grills
www.weber.com

(Zefirro makes a masonry wood and charcoal grill and pizza oven)
www.zefirro.com

Charcoal Roasting Box

Caja de China
  www.lacajachina.com

Composite Wood Decking and Rail Systems

ARTISAN rail system and TREX decking
  www.trex.com

Eon
  www.eonoutdoor.com

Epoch EverGrain Decking
  www.evergrain.com

Timber Tech
  www.timbertech.com

Veranda Deck
  www.verandadeck.com

Cooking with Wood, Fireplace Cookery

William Rubel, the author of *The Magic of Fire*, offers lots of advice and information about traditional fire cooking
www.williamrubel.com

www.spitjack.com sells tuscan grills and other tools for fireplace cookery, as well as leather gloves and hearth grills.

Countertops

Corian
  www.corian.com

Sheldon Slate
  www.sheldonslate.com

Steel and copper counters
  www.frigodesign.com

Vermont Soapstone
  www.vermontsoapstone.com

Cooking Wood

Maine Cooking Woods, LLC
  www.mainecookingwoods.com

Cupolas

www.cupolas.com

www.weathervane.com

www.architecturaldepot.com

Grill Pads

Diversitech Grill Pads
  www.diversitech.com

Electric Grills

Evo
  http://evo.leisuremax.us

MasterBuilt
  www.masterbuilt.com

Fans

Emerson outdoor fans
  www.fanshack.com

Hunter outdoor fans
  www.hunterfan.com

Modern architectural fans
  www.modernfan.com

Fireplaces

Hargrove Manufacturing Corporation
  www.hargrovegaslogs.com

Fire Stone Wood Burning Outdoor Fireplaces
  www.firestoneHP.com

Fire Pits

Agio Patio Embers
  www.agio-usa.com

O. W. Lee Co. Outdoor Hearth and Fire Pits
  (800) 776-9533

Gas Grills and Smokers

Altima Infrared Brick-Oven Grill
  www.sureheat.com

American Traditions
  www.islandbar-b-ques.com

Broil King
  www.broilkingbbq.com

Bubba's Bar-B-Q Ovens, Inc.
  www.bubbasovens.com

Bull Outdoor Products
  www.bullbbq.com

Cal Flame
  www.calspas.com

Capital Gas Grills
  www.capital-cooking.com

CFM Specialty Home Products— Vermont Castings Signature Gas Grills
  www.myownbbq.com
  www.vermontcastings.com

The Coleman Company
  www.coleman.com

DTG Sales Co. Electri-Chef Flameless Electric Outdoor Grills
  www.electri-chef.com

Dynasty Outdoor Grills by Jade Products Company
  www.dynastygrills.com

Evo Flattop Grill
  www.evoamerica.com

The Holland Grill
  www.hollandgrill.com

Jackson Grills Inc.
  www.jacksongrills.com

KitchenAid
  www.kitchenaid.com

Lynx Professional Grills
  www.lynxgrills.com

Napoleon Fireplaces and Grills
  www.napoleonfireplaces.com

Primo Kamodo-Style Gas Grill
  www.primogrill.com

Solaire Infrared Grilling Systems
www.rasmussen.biz

Sterling Forge Designer Stainless
Steel Gas Grills
www.sterlingforgegrills.com

Tec Infra-Red Grills
www.tecinfrared.com

Viking Range Corporation
www.vikingrange.com

Vintage Luxury Cooking Appliances
(800) 998-8966

Weber Grills
www.weber.com

Gas Grill Hookup

Maxitrol Company
www.plug1.com

Landscape Professionals

Edwin de Bruijn (designed the
Krasner gardens)
Hollands Bloom
Brattleboro, VT
(802)254-6965

Terrence Parker, ASLA
Terra Firma
Portsmouth, NH
www.terrafirmalandarch.com

Van Zelst Landscape Architects
Wadsworth, IL
(847) 623-3580

Lighting

Intermatic Professional Landscape
Lighting
www.intermatic.com

Kichler Lighting
www.kichler.com

Vista Professional Outdoor Lighting
www.vistapro.com

www.elights.com

www.lightingdirect.com

www.fiverivers.com

www.lightingshowplace.com

Masonry Ovens

Earthstone
www.earthstoneovens.com

Fogazzo Wood Fired Ovens &
BBQs
www.fogazzo.com

Forno Bravo
www.fornobravo.com

Le Panyol Ovens
www.mainewoodheat.com

Mugnaini
www.mugnaini.com

Pappa'z Pizza Oven
www.pizzaoven.co.za

Prairie Plus
www.soapstonetops.com/outdoor
kitchens.html

Alan Scott Custom Ovens
www.ovencrafters.net

Outdoor Cart

Standard Duty Utility Cart #311
www.elakeside.com

Outdoor Kitchen Specialists

This is a new specialty, so consult
your local hearth and patio
retailer and local kitchen show-
rooms for recommendations in
your area.

Designer Outdoor Kitchens (Kansas
City area)
Dick Atkins, designer
(913) 492-1255
Showroom, (913) 888-8028

Tom Nicolai
Prairie Plus (Chicago)
www.soapstonetops.com

Von Dreele-Freerksen Construction
(Chicago)
(708) 848-4130 or (708) 822-3461

Outdoor Sound Speakers

Bose
www.bose.com

Niles Audio
www.nilesaudio.com

Outdoor Kitchen Accessories

Alfie Thermal carafe
www.alficarafes.com

Bodum Glasses and Appliances
www.bodumusa.com

Brabantia waste storage
www.brabantia.com

Calphalon Contemporary Cutlery
www.calphalon.com

Charcoal Companion Barbecue
Tools and Accessories
www.companion-group.com

The Designers Edge BBQ Grill or
Workbench Utility Light
www.designersedge.com

Grillslinger Barbeque Tool System
www.grillslinger.com

KitchenAid Pots and Pans, Knives,
Barbecue Tools
www.kitchenaid.com

Oxo GoodGrips Houseware
Accessories
www.oxo.com

Simple Human Step Trash Cans and
Kitchen Accessories
www.simplehuman.com

Thermos Lunch Kits and Containers
www.thermos.com

Typhoon International Group, Ltd.
www.typhooneurope.com

Vic Firth Gourmet peppermills,
salt shakers, and rolling pins
www.vicfirthgourmet.com

Wilton Armetale Serveware
www.armetale.com

Patio Heaters

Dynamic Cooking Systems
www.dcsappliances.com

Endless Summer Patio Heater
Blue Rhino, available at
www.bluerhino.com

Solaira All-Season Outdoor Quartz
Heater
www.solairaheaters.com

Sterling Forge Premium Patio
Heaters
www.sterlingforgegrills.com

Pellet Grills

Traeger Pellet Grills
www.Traegerindustries.com

Pergolas, Gazebos, Arbors, Sheds

www.amishcountrygazebos.com

www.backyardamerica.com

www.baldwinpergolas.com

www.jamaicacottage.com

www.newenglandarbors.com

www.summerwood.com

www.vixenhill.com

Refrigerators and Beverage Centers

DCS
www.dcsappliances.com

KitchenAid
www.kitchenaid.com

Marvel
www.marvelindustries.com

Summit
www.summitappliance.com

Twin Eagles, Inc.
www.twineaglesbbq.com

Viking
www.vikingrange.com

Shading Systems

King Canopy, Powel & Powel
Supply Co.
www.kingcanopy.com

www.shade-sails.com

www.shadesystemsinc.com

Sinks

Luxury Home Products (copper
sinks)
www.luxuryhomeproducts.com

Sheldon Slate (slate sinks)
www.sheldonslate.com

Vermont Soapstone
www.vermontsoapstone.com

Smokers, Electric

Bradley Smoker
www.bradleysmoker.com

Brinkmann Smokers
www.brinkmann.net

Cookshack Outdoor Smoker
www.cookshack.com

Stone

Granite Gold Fine Granite and
Stone Care Products
www.granitegold.com

Natural Stone Veneers
International, LLC
www.nsvi.com

Owens Corning Cultured Stone
www.owenscorning.com

Underdeck Systems

www.backyardamerica.com

www.decksandthings.com

www.undercoversystems.com

Warming Drawers

Dacor
www.dacor.com

KitchenAid
www.kitchenaid.com

Twin Eagles, Inc.
www.twineaglesbbq.com

Viking
www.vikingrange.com

Vintage Luxury Cooking
Appliances
(800) 998-8966

Websites for a Variety of Products within Categories

Countertop and Cooking

www.ikea.com (large outdoor
planters as well as kitchen
equipment)

www.napastyle.com (cooking and
serving)

www.wisteria.com (outdoor furniture, candle lights, serving bowls,
decorative)

Gardening

Gardener's Supply Company
(general garden tools, equipment)
www.gardeners.com

McClure & Zimmerman (bulbs)
www.mzbulb.com

Smith and Hawkins (general garden
tools, equipment)
www.smithandhawkins.com

Van Engelen bulbs
www.vanengelen.com

www.frenchgardening.com
(English language site for French herb, vegetable, and wildflower seeds, garden tools and accessories, garden lighting and tabletop)

Miscellaneous Products

SBCFiremaster Bee Free Wasp Deterrent
sales@sbcfiremaster.com

SkeeterVAC Propane Fueled Bug System
www.skeetervac.com

Blue Rhino
www.bluerhino.com

SimpleFire, LLC Firestarters
www.simplefire.com

SureFire Vented Gas Logs
www.sureheat.com

Sautee Cedar Company Grilling Planks
www.sauteecedar.com

SAVU Smoker Bags
www.savu.fi

Products and Sources for Vermont Demonstration Kitchen

Appliances
KitchenAid: 36 in. gas grill, double side burners with griddle and wok attachments, undercounter refrigerator
The Big Green Egg: charcoal grill
CookShack: undercounter electric smoker
Fogazzo: wood-burning masonry oven, covered in white stucco, with soapstone shelf and slate apron

Bar Stools, Tables, Chairs, Chaise Longues, Sofa, Armchairs
Carter Grandle Casual Furniture

Cabinets for the Outdoor Kitchen
Danver: stainless steel outdoor kitchen cabinets

Cedar Roof Shingles
Teal Cedar

Ceiling Fans
The Modern Fan Company: galvanized industry fans on screen porch and in kitchen pavilion

Contractor
Jim Spencer
TrueCraft Construction
Newfane, VT

Counters, Eating Bar, and Apron-Front Sink
Vermont Soapstone

Countertop Appliances and Accessories
Cutting board: custom wood mosaic, from Grothouse Lumber, www.glumber.com

Vita Mix blender
KitchenAid pots, pans, chef's knives, food processor, barbecue tools
Typhoon scale and tea kettle

Cupola on Outdoor Kitchen Pavilion
www.weathervane.com

Deck
Trex decking with Artisan Rail system, www.trex.com

Design Credits
ARCHITECTURE:
Andy Armstrong
Renovation Architect
Armstrong and Associates
P.O. Box 820
Roswell, GA 30077
(770)967-3296
armstrarch@aol.com

LANDSCAPE DESIGN:
Edwin deBruijn
Hollands Bloom
1029 Upper Dummerston Rd.
Brattleboro, VT 05301

LIGHTING DESIGN:
Thomas Petrush
Vista Professional Landscape Lighting
www.vistapro.com

KITCHEN DESIGN:
Deborah Krasner
Kitchens for Cooks
www.kitchensforcooks.net

Faucet
Chicago Faucet: articulating wall-mount model in brushed nickel

Fountain
Wall fountain from Krupps
www.krupps.com

Insect Control
SkeeterVac by Blue Rhino

Lighting
Vista Professional Outdoor Lighting (outdoor kitchen, paths, deck)
Kichler Lighting (two wall sconces on deck)

Patio Heater
Endless Summer by Blue Rhino

Pavers
Ardennes Grey Bergerac by Belgard

Planters
Campagnia International

Porch Screen System
ScreenMobile

Pressure-Treated Wood
Wolmanized Lumber

Skylight on Porch
Velux

Sound System Outdoor Speakers
Niles Audio

Index

Credits

p. 2: © Chipper Hatter

p. 4: © Chipper Hatter

p. 5: © Lee Anne White

p. 6 © Rob Karosis

p. 7: © Lee Anne White

p. 8: © Ken Gutmaker

p. 9: ©Brian Vanden Brink, Photographer 2006

p. 10: © Lee Anne White

p. 11: top: © Brian Vanden Brink, Photographer 2006, Design: Elliot Elliot Norelius Architects; bottom: © www.tonysears.com

p. 14: © Scott Zimmerman

p. 15: © Lisa Romerein

p. 16: top: © www.tonysears.com; bottom: © Brian Vanden Brink, Photographer 2006, Design: Hutker Architects

p. 17: © Ben Fink

p. 19: top: © Lee Anne White; bottom: © Lynn Karlin

p. 20: © Saxon Holt

p. 21: © Grey Crawford

p. 22: © Linda Svendsen

p. 28: © Lee Anne White

p. 34: © Brian Vanden Brink, Photographer 2006

pp. 50–53: © Brian Vanden Brink, Photographer 2006, Design: Ellen Levinson Interiors

p. 56: Bottom: © Lisa Romerein

p. 59: Bottom: Photo courtesy Kingsford

p. 60: Photo courtesy Big Green Egg

p. 61: Top: Photo courtesy Traeger Grills; Bottom: Photo courtesy Portable Kitchens, Inc.

p. 63: Photo courtesy TEC

p. 64: © Lisa Romerein

p. 65: Top: Photo courtesy KitchenAid; Bottom: © Linda Oyama Bryan for Van Zelst, Inc.

p. 66: © Linda Svendsen

p. 67: Courtesy Evo, Inc.

p. 68: Top: Photo courtesy Masterbuilt; Bottom: © Ken Gutmaker

p. 70: Top: © Scott Zimmerman

p. 72: © Linda Oyama Bryan for Van Zelst, Inc.

p. 73: Top: © Scott Zimmerman

p. 74: Photo courtesy Caja China

p. 75: © Scott Zimmerman

p. 86-91: All photos © Linda Oyama Bryan for Van Zelst, Inc.

p. 98: © Lisa Romerein

p. 99: © Lee Anne White

p. 100: top: © Ken Gutmaker; bottom: © Randy Guyer

p. 103: © Lee Anne White

p. 104: top: © Lee Anne White; bottom: courtesy KitchenAid

p. 105: Photo courtesy KCA

p. 106: top: © Ken Gutmaker; bottom: © Ben Fink

p. 108: © Ben Fink

p. 110: © Lee Anne White

p. 111: top: © Scott Zimmerman

p. 113: © Scott Zimmerman

p. 134: © Brian Vanden Brink, Photographer 2006; Design: Horiuchi & Solien Landscape Architects

p. 135: © Linda Oyama Bryan for Van Zelst, Inc.

p. 136: © Don Ipock

p. 137: Top: © Scott Zimmerman; Bottom: © Lee Anne White

p. 138: © Rob Karosis

p. 139: Left: © Brian Vanden Brink, Photographer 2006; Right: © Scott Zimmerman

p. 140: © Lisa Romerein

p. 141: © Rob Karosis

p. 142: © Brian Vanden Brink, Photographer 2006

p. 143: Top and bottom: © Tim Street Porter

p. 144: Scottt Zimmerman

p. 145: © Lee Anne White

p. 146: Top left: Photo courtesy Three Birds; top right: © Brian Vanden Brink, Photographer 2006; Design: Weatherend Estate Furniture; bottom left and right: © Lisa Romerein

p. 147: Top: © Ken Gutmaker

p. 148: Top right: © Lisa Romerein

p. 149: © Lisa Romerein

p. 150: © Scott Zimmerman

p. 151: Top: © Tim Street-Porter, bottom: Photo courtesy Skeetervac

p. 152: © Lynn Karlin

p. 153: © Scott Zimmerman

p. 154: © Tim Street-Porter

p. 155: Top: © Lisa Romerein; bottom: © Tim Street-Porter

p. 156: Top: © Rob Karosis; bottom: © Scott Zimmerman

p. 157: © Lee Anne White

p. 182: © Lisa Romerein

p. 183: © Lynn Karlin

p. 184: © Robert Perron

p. 185: © Brian Vanden Brink, Photographer 2006; Design: Horiuchi & Solein Landscape Architects

p. 187: © Scott Zimmerman

p. 188: © Brian Vanden Brink, Photographer 2006; Design: Robinson & Grisaru Architects

p. 189: © Robert Perron

p. 190: © Scott Zimmerman

p. 191: © Brian Vanden Brink, Photographer 2006

pp. 193–194: © Lee Anne White

p. 195: © Todd Caverly

pp. 196–197: © Lynn Karlin

p. 199: © Lynn Karlin

p. 201: © Brian Vanden Brink, Photographer 2006; Design: Horiuchi & Solein Landscape Architects

p. 202: © Lynn Karlin

p. 203: © Brian Vanden Brink, Photographer 2006; Design: Horiuchi & Solein Landscape Architects

p. 205: © Brian Vanden Brink, Photographer 2006; Design: Polhemus Savery DaSilva Architects